DO It

ᴽᴽ AND BE GLAD YOU DID ᴽᴽ

First Published by Aspen Ridge Books
ISBN 978-1-7332992-0-6

WRITTEN BY	Shauna Ganes of the *Do It and Be Glad You Did* Podcast
EDITED BY	Lori Brown Patrick, the Grammarwitch
ILLUSTRATED BY	Jarod Roselló, author of *Red Panda & Moon Bear*
BOOK DESIGN BY	Adam Robinson for Good Book Developers

Please visit www.shaunaganes.com

Disclaimer: Real estate laws and regulations vary from state to state and market to market. Always consult your local governing bodies to be clear about all the laws and rules for real estate where you will be practicing. The examples in this book are largely specific to Nevada law and may not be applicable in your market.

DO IT AND BE GLAD YOU DID

A Not-Stodgy Business Book About
What It Takes to Make It in Real Estate

Shauna Ganes

Aspen Ridge Books
Reno, NV

Introduction

Part the First: Know Before You Go

15   Chapter 1
The Basics/Buyer Beware

If you're thinking of getting into real estate, here's what you should know ... career or hobby? ... dealing with other agents ... writing a good offer ... standards of practice and professionalism ... the nitty-gritty of independence ... liability and accountability ... new home sales vs. resale

Part the Second: The Right Stuff

29   Chapter 2
Choosing a Broker

Your license needs a home ... different characteristics of brokers ... do your homework ... good reputation ... up to date on market trends and conditions ... attentive to agents ... committed to professionalism ... professional history ... cost structure ... monthly fees and sales commissions ... compatible office environment

35   Chapter 3
Professional Image: Setting Your Own High Bar

The bar to entry is low; set the bar high for yourself ... creating a professional image: communication, attire, passive communication, office environment, honesty, courtesy, accountability

49 Chapter 4
Choosing a Mentor

Finding a mentor ... you'll need a Yoda to talk things
through when stuff gets weird ... do the right thing ...
qualities of a good mentor ... listen to your Spidey-sense

Part the Third: The Rock (bedrock, that is)

55 Chapter 5
Choosing a Business Model

What kind of business do you want? ... pinpoint your geographical
market ... choices: buyers/sellers, luxury/everything else,
ranches/suburban, commercial/residential ... relevant
professional designations ... your professional boundaries

63 Chapter 6
Professional Boundaries

Making room for your life ...defining your availability ... leveraging
technology to reinforce boundaries ... handling difficult clients
... when and how to walk away ... listening to your gut feeling

67 Chapter 7
*Creating a Business Plan: Foundational
Ideology, Strategic Plan, and Budget*

The Book ... personal standards of practice ... business plan ...
core ideology ... mission, inspiration, culture, beliefs, expectations,
strategic planning, funnels of business, lead generation ...
budgeting, tracking, and data ... office overhead, commission
splits, and referral fees ... CPAs and attorneys ... business entity

79　　Chapter 8
　　　Systems and Procedures

　　　Develop systems and procedures manual ... every deal follows
　　　the same basic steps ... staying on top of purchase contract
　　　deadlines ... checklists ... client database ... desk/office
　　　setup ... How do you organize? ... routines for success

Part the Fourth: Be Your Best Self and Retain More Business

87　　Chapter 9
　　　Personal and Professional Development, Plus Networking

　　　Continuing education, relevant designations, the company you keep
　　　... influences ... staying on top of industry trends, market values,
　　　and forecasting ... national vs. local market data ... farming ... head
　　　trash vs. a positive mindset ... budgeting for coaching, conventions,
　　　and seminars ... What does networking look like for you?

97　　Chapter 10
　　　Prospecting

　　　Client attraction and retention ... your sphere of influence ...
　　　funnels for leads ... farming, open houses, drip campaigns ...
　　　lead-generation tools ... transactional or relational? Know thyself:
　　　lead generation that fits your personality ... pop-bys, client parties,
　　　notes, calls, silver bullets, inside sales agents, online leads, open
　　　houses, billboards, radio ads, social media, targeted ads ... keeping
　　　your marketing professional ... tracking and spreadsheets

Part the Fifth: Something Bigger Than Yourself

107   Chapter 11
        Your Team and Network

        Little black book of vendors ... building an external team
        ... lenders, escrow and title professionals, inspectors,
        financial advisors, accountants, attorneys, contractors,
        landscapers, and other vendors ... getting and making
        referrals ... building your internal team ... hiring

119   Chapter 12
        Self-care

        Avoiding burnout ... budget for vacations ... weekends
        ... exercise ... protecting your personal boundaries

123   Chapter 13
        What's Next?

        Acknowledgments
        Author Bio

To Kimberley Elliot for guiding me through the fog and helping me find my captain.

To my husband, Bryce,
for being the best cheerleader a girl could hope for.

INTRODUCTION

Who I am ... a bit of my history in real estate ... why I'm writing a book ... my vision and intention for the book, and what to expect ... What does "professionalism" mean? What does it look like?

I'm never moving back to Reno and I'm never working for my dad.

Well, never say never. After graduating from college and then graduating from culinary school, I took a job offer I had sworn myself against as a teenager. Fast-forward over 10 years and I'm still here!

My dad is kind of a big deal in our area. He's been in the real estate business for over 40 years and earned every award in the RE/MAX organization, including the Circle of Legends Award and Luminary of Distinction (RE/MAX's highest honor). Go, Dad!

Having him as my mentor expedited my education. It was very "sink or swim." In a trial-by-fire environment, and within the stresses of the economic downturn of 2008, it felt as though I had gained years of experience in a matter of months, and other agents with vastly more experience than I were asking my advice on how to proceed in a transaction. That was interesting.

Now that I've been on the real estate roller coaster for over a decade, I've caught myself reflecting more on the industry as a whole and recognizing that real estate sales agents, on the whole, do not have a stellar reputation. Popular TV and movies often poke fun at us, showing us as neurotic people-pleasers, good-hearted zombies, or sleazy money-grubbers. Pass!

That public image causes a lot of consumers to have little or no respect for real estate agents, and it shows. Un-fun. But if we want to be treated as the professionals we know ourselves to be, we have to act like it—every day.

My vision is to raise the playing field by helping real estate professionals everywhere elevate their game. It inspired me to start a podcast called *Do It and Be Glad You Did* (available on podcast platforms everywhere) to reach as many ears as possible and start a broad conversation about professionalism and how to approach this business "right."

My way is not The Way. I am sharing A Way to approach real estate. In all my observations over the years, I have noticed that agents who operate from a business foundation and mindset tend to be the most successful agents in the market. Those who approach real estate as a hobby, side job, or just a way to make quick cash in a hot market tend to fizzle out as soon as the market shifts and gets "hard."

The low barrier to entry is the culprit, in my mind. How do you set yourself apart from the thousands of other agents in your market and give your business the best chance for success? If you are holding this book, you are likely considering real estate as a career and would like to be in business 10 years from now.

If you want that longevity and success, then you need to think of real estate as a business and yourself as a professional.

The following chapters tackle the question, "What does professionalism mean, and what does it look like in practice?" I'll cover everything from what you should know before deciding to get a real estate license to what you should consider when designing a business model, and more.

Consider yourself a Padawan, and this book is your Yoda.

CHAPTER 1

THE BASICS/BUYER BEWARE

*If you're thinking of getting into real estate, here's what you
should know ... career or hobby? ... dealing with other
agents ... writing a good offer ... standards of practice
and professionalism ... the nitty-gritty of independence ...
liability and accountability ... new home sales vs. resale*

So you're thinking of getting a real estate license? Let's chat ...

I'm often approached by friends and acquaintances who are interested in getting into real estate and want to know what it's like and probably want to be offered a job on our team. I'm always happy to have such conversations and paint a realistic picture of what the residential real estate sales industry is like. People have such a glamorous idea of what it's like to be a Realtor, and they never consider what the business really looks like without makeup and accessories.

All too often, the person expressing interest thinks it's an easy way to make money. They think they'd be good at it because they love to look at homes. Ha! If my job was just about showing houses and giving decorating tips, I'd be a zillionaire.

Beware, ye who enter here. There's so much more to this business than meets the eye. The level of communication skills you need is bananas, not to mention the organizational skill to manage a lot of moving parts across varying timelines. Have a short fuse? Get it in check, because losing your temper will not serve you here. You also need good business acumen, or a partner or trusted advisor with said acumen, to guide you on such things, since you are running your own small business.

When people don't treat their foray into real estate as a business, that's where the cracks start to show. There's no Coast Guard for wayward real estate agents to save you. You're on your own, kid.

Consider, first, the cost of entry. Do you have an extra $10,000 lying around? Seriously, add up what it costs to:

- go to real estate school (or to buy the book to learn at home);
- take the test (in Nevada it's $100 a pop, and you can take the test as many times as needed until you pass);
- pay for your license;
- pay for access to the MLS;

- pay National Association of Realtor dues (if you decide to become a Realtor);
- pay dues to your local real estate board;
- pay for any software or other tech you need to get set up (i.e., lockboxes and access tools, desktop computer, laptop, or tablet, transaction management system, etc.);
- pay any fees your broker may charge to bring you on board (some brokers will just take a chunk of each commission you earn until you pay them back each year to cover your office fees; others charge a monthly fee to the agents);
- pay for business cards and a website.

Whew! Now that you've potentially lost an arm and a leg (remember, you haven't earned a dime yet, so that money is coming from somewhere else and you're living off your savings for now), are you stoked to spend the next 30-90 days:

- prospecting to get your first lead;
- putting in all the work it takes to get that lead into contract;
- go through the twists and turns of the escrow process to a (hopefully) successful closing;
- and then get paid with whatever is left after your broker takes their portion?

No? Okay, that's cool. It was a pleasure to meet you. Yes? Rock on, my friend. Keep reading.

Next, ask yourself: Do I want to go into real estate as a hobby or a career? There's a huge difference between the two, not just in levels of success and income, but in the level of professionalism, experience, and value to a client.

Option A: Hobbyist. A hobbyist is often a person who:

- has a spouse who earns a stable, healthy income to support the household, where all the money earned from the other partner's sales commissions is either fun money or goes into the family savings pool;
- or is retired;

- or has other income that pays their bills;
- or just wants something to keep them busy and their mind sharp.

Option B: Career Real Estate Professional. Simply, this means you choose to have real estate be your career and treat it like a business, of which you are the owner. You'd better put on your big-kid pants and get ready for some serious business planning and work, because the scary part of real estate is that there's no paycheck coming your way every two weeks like clockwork. If you don't hustle and stay on top of lead-generation activities (i.e., creating business), your pipeline will dry up like the desert and leave you stranded. There is no lifeboat here, people. Not sounding awesome? Turn back now. Getting pumped? Let's continue.

Neither of these is a bad thing. In fact, both sound delightful and highlight one of the beautiful things about real estate: it's flexible! The important thing is to consider the question in the first place. Your business planning will be quite different, depending on which path you choose. So choose wisely, young Skywalker.

Ensure that you can withstand a cyclical industry where feast and famine is really common. Will you be able to stick to an operating budget and sock money away during the "feast" so you don't panic and file for unemployment during a "famine"? You can tell when someone new to the business, especially, isn't adhering to their budget while riding high on the hog during a great streak, because they'll show up at work with a fancy new car or go on some expensive vacation, all the while forgetting that they won't have anything in the pipeline next month and then crashing down into freak-out mode.

The market crash of 2008 was terrifying for a lot of agents, and they jumped ship because homes were losing value at an alarming rate, especially in Florida, Michigan, Arizona, Nevada, and California, and deals were really hard. On the bright side, it culled out the people who had gotten into the industry when it was super easy to sell a house and prices were insanely high, so the return was amazing. They couldn't hang when the going got tough and you actually needed skills to get a listing and keep a deal together. Short sales, how I don't miss you.

Prospecting isn't sexy, but it's what keeps your pipeline full and your income flowing. My dad is a transactional personality, and I am relational. As a result, our prospecting can look very different. He's great at making lots of calls and shaking deals from the trees, whereas I'm involved in Rotary, Children's Miracle Network Hospitals, and a bunch of other social things that keep me in touch with my sphere of influence, and I am grateful for the business that has been generated out of such associations.

You need to really dig and be straight with yourself about what kind of person you are. Not only in personality and simple things like whether you are an introvert or an extrovert, but also in things like how you respond to expectation and pressure. Author Gretchen Rubin (gretchenrubin.com) has a phenomenal accountability framework that addresses, with Four Tendencies, how people respond to outer versus inner expectations. To offer context, an outer expectation is a work deadline, while an inner expectation is a New Year's resolution or fitness goal.

Rubin's Four Tendencies are Upholder, Obliger, Questioner, and Rebel. I'm a Questioner, which in her framework means that I will follow through on either inner or outer expectations; I just have to know why. There's a great motto for this tendency: "Tell me why, and I'll comply." That speaks to me.

Take the quiz at *quiz.gretchenrubin.com* to find out your tendency.

Knowing how you respond to things like inner and outer expectations will help you create structures that keep you on task and aid in your success. For example, if you were an Obliger, the kind of person who needs a lot of outer accountability in order to get things done, it would be a really bad idea to work from home, where there's no sense of outer accountability because no one ever sees you. That being said, if working from home is a must and you still need that outer accountability, I would strongly encourage setting up deadlines for projects with a coach or business partner, so you know someone else is relying on you to get something done. If no one is counting on you to prospect and make 50 calls a week and you know you won't just do it for yourself, what are you going to put in place to make sure you follow through?

If you're thinking big and see yourself leading a whole team, it is extra helpful to know how your teammates think and operate, so you can foster harmony among your team members and create optimal workflow.

Emergenetics is another fantastic resource. It breaks the brain down into four major quadrants (Conceptual, Social, Structural, and Analytical) and plots behavioral characteristics across three attributes (Expressiveness, Assertiveness, and Flexibility) *www.emergenetics.com*. When you not only know how you operate but how those you work with operate, it creates amazing synergy and avoids unpleasant clashes that distract you from your true goal: productivity.

More often than not, a newly licensed agent is going out on their own and not joining an established team. Either way, you need to know these things about yourself. And don't be afraid to ask the team lead, who may be interested in hiring you, if they use DiSC, Emergenetics, the Buffini Heritage Profile, or something else to better understand how each team member operates, to ensure they are a good fit for you, too.

A friend of mine is an architect. At his firm, everyone has their Emergenetics profile posted outside their cubicle, so you can effectively code-switch when speaking to them. Speaking to someone in their language? What a novel concept.

PLAYING WELL WITH OTHERS

Another big part of real estate is dealing with other real estate agents. I'm shocked and saddened at how often conversations with other agents go sideways because of arrogance, ignorance, or the blindness of taking on their client's emotions as their own.

As a real estate professional, you are your client's advocate. You are there to help guide them through a complicated process, mitigate their liability, and keep their best interests at the forefront of everything you do. When a deal gets hinky, it's in no way helpful to get just as mad or frustrated as the client and then take that out on the other agent. That does not bring resolution; it just pisses people off.

Instead, you need to be able to acknowledge your client's feelings while maintaining your objective position as their advocate and helping them make good decisions. That can even mean telling a client something they don't want to hear, but it's critical that they honor their obligations under the contract, or else they're looking at unpleasant consequences. Sometimes, the good decision is letting a deal go. Don't force something together because you need a paycheck. Not cool, not ethical. The Dude would not abide.

One way to keep yourself in an objective advocate mindset is to check your vocabulary. When you're talking about, or to, a client, are you saying things like "we" when you're really meaning "you"? I hear that a lot: "We received a stupid offer and we're going to reject." Huh? We didn't do that. When you talk like you're the one in the deal, you're destined to get into the weeds emotionally. That takes you out of being an advocate and a professional and puts you into being an echo chamber of the client's emotions and fears. That's not a place where rational thought happens and problems are solved; it just exacerbates the rage monster who wants to crush everything in sight. Don't feed that guy.

GETTING OFF ON THE RIGHT FOOT

The other kind of conversation I've seen kick off the receipt of an offer on a downhill slide is immediate arrogance with a know-it-all attitude. If you're sending an email (in which tone cannot be heard) that comes across as pushy, inconsiderate, or rude, that is never a good thing. But it's especially bad when it's the first communication you're sending a listing agent that includes an offer. Remember that you're going to have to work with that other person for the next four solid weeks or more and also work together to overcome any issues. It can really sour a deal if the first impression you make is a bad one. Always be the consummate professional. Nobody really cares how many deals you have or have not done if you wrote a bad offer from the get-go.

A "bad offer" can look all kinds of ways: unreasonably low price, blank sections within the offer, mismatched timelines, unreasonable additional requests, or—one of my favorites—a really low purchase price and also a request for the seller to pay the buyer's closing costs. My dad calls that "discounting the discount"—when a buyer wants a steal on the price and also wants the seller to give up more of that low price by paying for the buyer's costs to close (i.e., inspection bills, escrow fee, transfer tax, HOA transfer fees, and so on).

Sometimes this happens because the agent who wrote the offer doesn't understand what the contract says in the first place, or they created a bad habit somewhere along the way and have been repeating the same craziness ever since. What it usually looks like is terrible contract language that is in no way clear or intelligible.

You can also see issues with an offer come up when a real estate board updates the contract to include new language, take out old language, or even update signing blocks, etc. Even an agent who has been in the business for decades can make these rookie mistakes of writing bad offers when they don't take the time to review the changes and ensure they understand them, or worse, they use the old form, instead of writing an offer on the proper, updated form. That last bit might seem like it's not a big deal, but your broker's E&O (Errors and Omissions) Insurance feels quite differently. If you've just given up the protections of that insurance because you, the real estate professional, didn't use the proper document, you're going to kick yourself. Hard.

Hopefully you have a great broker who will bring such contract changes to your attention in an office meeting and answer any questions you may have before you start using the new forms. More on that later.

Double-check the offers you write to be sure they are complete and that any special terms or conditions that have been added are clear. Think of this when approached with a unique term your client wants in a contract: Who does what by when, and what happens if they don't? If you can answer all of those questions, you've written a good clause. Otherwise you risk confusion on the other party's behalf, and if there are no consequences for not following through on the requested item, your client has no recourse against the other side, who didn't perform as requested.

Blanks are not acceptable! If your client expects certain fixtures or personal property to stay with the house after closing, *put it in writing.*

> TEACHABLE MOMENT: Ambiguity benefits no one. When in doubt, spell it out.

When you go to real estate school, or learn via correspondence, you don't actually learn anything about the practice of real estate. You just learn how to pass a test. (I've heard the same is true of law school.) Once you have your license, who's there to show you the ropes, and how do you know that person even knows what they are doing? Enter the wide spectrum of standards of practice and professionalism.

One thing that's in your control: your ability to read. Simply reading through a purchase agreement, from start to finish, will tell you everything you need to know about how to formulate a basic offer and what steps need to be taken to get you to a successful closing. It has all the deadlines and expectations right there, in black and white. The fun part is all the crazy stuff that can happen in between and what it takes to write a "good offer."

Obviously, opinions about what makes a good offer vary, but I do think there are key elements that create an offer that is "uncounterable," so to speak. The thing about that is, you have to be willing to think like a seller. Being a bully in a negotiation is rude and ineffective. It's also not negotiating at that point; it's demanding. Don't be shocked if the other party is turned off by that and tells your client to pound sand.

Instead, if you look at an offer from both sides of the table, you'll be able to draft something beautiful that isn't argued and negotiate a deal that will be much more likely to flow smoothly. My favorite scenario (not!) is when a buyer wants to look at houses and make offers that are contingent on the sale of their home—a home they haven't even listed yet. 1) It is a discourtesy to the seller to inconvenience them with a showing, after which they are always hopeful an offer will come in, and 2) the buyer isn't actually in a position to buy or at least negotiate on firm footing. As a seller, how psyched would you be to find out you took the time to get your home presentable for a potential buyer who isn't really in a position to buy your home? Even if a contingent buyer does decide to pitch an offer, as a seller, how much would you really want to take your home off the market while you wait for the buyer to get their home listed, attract an acceptable offer, and go through their due diligence so you can have confidence that your buyer's sale will actually go through? See all the dominoes here?

Even with that brief example, how is a noob supposed to understand the nuance of such an agreement and how to counsel their client wisely on an appropriate response? Also, if you're the one receiving a complicated offer with funky contingencies that you don't understand, will you have the humility to ask the other agent what they mean? Will you blindly go along with it and have your clients agree to something you don't even understand and can't explain? Will you yell at the other agent to cover up your own ignorance? I've seen all of those happen.

Enter scary liability spiel: if you don't understand something and have your client agree to it anyway and they also don't understand and it results in damages to them, *you are liable and will suffer the consequences.*

NO SAFETY NET

Another fun reminder, aside from there's no guaranteed paycheck and you're working for free until a deal closes, is that there's no guaranteed retirement package. Your broker is not responsible for providing you a 401(k) and polishing a gold watch to hand over to you when you decide to retire. Wouldn't that be something!

Instead, all of that future planning is on you, pal. If that freaks you out or really turns you off, stop reading now and enjoy another career path that offers financial security and retirement planning.

Later in this book I'll cover exciting things like budgets and how to plan for your future in this business. I got you, boo!

CYA ALL DAY

One of the scariest things we deal with is liability. Not only our own, but that of our clients as well. We have to know the contract, risks, and obligations well enough to keep ourselves out of trouble, but also to protect our clients from risk. We have a fiduciary responsibility to them, not to mention ethical commitments, and we have to maneuver through that with every new deal. Every state is different, but keep in mind they all have rules that also govern your marketing, and they will be watching you. Even if your local governing body misses a marketing violation you committed, your fellow agents will be quick to report it.

Real estate is one of the most highly regulated industries out there, but you would never think it to look at how some agents practice. We also have our own unique judicial system that allows infractions to be heard in front of a panel of, essentially, industry peers. Surely every state does it a little differently. The point is, there are enough rules specific to real estate, and enough infractions thereof, to constitute such a system. Having to appear in front of the Real Estate Commission sounds terrifying to me, not to mention embarrassing. In Nevada, if you go in front of the Commission and they rule against you, your booboo is announced in a monthly publication called The Open House. My stomach turns just thinking about it.

There are also state laws you have to abide by, and if you break one of those, the consequences are much more severe. We're not just talking about a fine and an embarrassing plug in The Open House. We're talking about career-ending consequences.

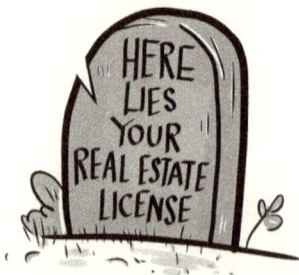

IT'S NOT APPLES TO APPLES

If you've done new home sales in the past and are considering making the switch to resale, know that it is not apples to apples. You will be confronted with all the issues and liabilities you didn't have working for a builder.

You'll certainly hit the ground running with a working knowledge of contracts and sales, but don't let that give you a false sense of security, because something will bite you in the butt to wake you up. Not fun.

If you haven't been scared off by now, let's continue on this Hero's Journey as you embark on a new professional adventure. Tallyho!

CHAPTER 2

CHOOSING A BROKER

*Your license needs a home ... different characteristics of brokers ...
do your homework ... good reputation ... up to date on market
trends and conditions ... attentive to agents ... committed to
professionalism ... professional history ... cost structure ... monthly
fees and sales commissions ... compatible office environment*

Let's say you've made it through the gauntlet of school and testing (of course you passed on the first try) and now you need a home for your license. (You can't let it flap in the breeze; you have to "hang your license" somewhere after you get it.) Be warned: not all brokers and brokerages are the same. Choose wisely, Indiana Jones. If you're really serious about taking on a career in real estate and becoming a stellar professional, let your first decision of where to start your practice be a great one, one that sets you on a path to success and places you in the orbit of established professionals you can learn from. Not that bad choice with shiny bobbles that turned the bad guy into the Crypt Keeper. So gross.

Take your time to interview brokers. Some are out just to rack up as many agents as possible and are not truly willing to invest in your success by offering top-notch training, tools, and guidance. Meanwhile, others do not take on newly licensed agents as a rule, because they are strictly focused on being a home for agents who are already successful and looking to boost their success and grow their business. If that sounds like where you want to be, keep that as part of your plan for growth. Start somewhere else that will guide you and support you and then work on elevating yourself to a higher level of brokerage to blow the roof off your business.

Ask a lot of questions and do whatever publicly available research you can about the broker. Remember, they are your guide and ultimately responsible for every deal in their office. Make sure they

- have a good reputation;
- stay on top of market trends and economic news that affects the real estate industry;
- frequently bring tools and trainings to their agents;
- have a firm commitment to risk reduction, ethics, and professionalism.

They are supposed to have your back and also be willing to hold you accountable if you're in the wrong. It helps you be a better agent. If a broker is always on your side, no matter what, that's not as awesome as it might seem. Having your back also means calling you on your shit.

Another thing to look out for is a broker who also actively sells real estate. No shade to those brokers out there who do this, I've just noticed that it distracts the broker from taking on their duties full force and puts them in direct competition with their own agents. Plus, if you ever have a deal with such a broker and it's not going well, due in large part to their poor communication or unprofessional behavior, who do you tell? It makes a difference when you're able to take a grievance to a broker to help iron out challenges instead of having to report them to your local board, which may be a bigger hammer than you really need to use.

I've also had deals with brokers who did not follow the deadlines and terms of the purchase agreement. We're all human, slack given, but one should expect a bit more from a broker, who is supposed to be a voice of reason, knowledge, and experience. Forgetting about the terms of a contract and delaying something like repairs is not an error you should be seeing from a broker, at least not an experienced one. Brokers use the contract as their bible and will always reference the agreement when there is an issue or dispute, which is another reason it is so important to write clear contract language and understand what the agreement says. It is also why you expect a broker who also actively sells to have a deep understanding of the document.

Every state is different, and you should check with your local licensing requirements to see what it takes to become a broker. The barrier to entry is low across the board, and a broker isn't much of an exception. Not to say there isn't more work, or a college degree involved, it's just that they don't have to have 20 years of real estate experience, an MBA, and a law degree.

When you're interviewing, ask about the broker's professional history. Note the requirements they cover and how much experience they have. Ask why and how they decided to become a broker. Who was their mentor? Did they have one? That story should be very telling.

Also consider cost structure. Some brokerages will charge agents a low monthly fee (or no monthly fee at all), but take a generous portion of your sales commissions after each closed transaction until you cover the overhead you owe to the broker each year. (The faster you do that, the faster you get a better split with the broker.) Other brokerages charge a steep monthly fee but take a very small, and in some cases no, percentage off the top of what you earn from each closing. The brokerage is a business, too, and the owners make their money from these various types of fee structures. In return, the agents get office space, marketing tools, training, copy services, coverage from the broker's E&O (errors and omissions) insurance, etc.

Knowing you're new, take cost effectiveness into account, compared to the resources and support offered in the office. If you have a certain nut to cover (i.e., the lump sum owed by each agent back to the broker to cover their costs), make sure you can achieve that fairly quickly in the year, so you can enjoy a higher split to you for the rest of the deals you close. If your business is slow to get going, you'll essentially be paying your broker back all year long and not enjoying much profit.

On the other hand, a brokerage that requires a monthly fee may—or may not—be a good choice for you if you are planning on hustling right out of the gate and have a great business plan in place to generate as much business as you can, as fast as possible. That would make a monthly fee potentially workable, if you plan for longevity and don't shine brightly for an instant and then fade like a sad fireworks show. If you have ample savings that can cover the financial commitment owed to your broker up front, that boosts your ability to enjoy a more beneficial split right away.

Conversely, if you'd prefer to dabble or try the hobbyist route and not have the stress of a high monthly financial commitment, you're better off with a brokerage that does not have said high monthly requirement and instead pays itself back from your earned commissions. Same thing if you're new to an area or generally don't have a sphere of influence to pull from and know your business will be a bit slower to get off the ground: stick with something that is more affordable to you for the first 12–24 months. You can always change ships later.

Some communities may also have unique brokerages that are basically the coat check of real estate, where a licensee can keep their license active and "hang" it with a brokerage that costs the agent nothing per month and the broker of record takes a very small fee with each closing. This is ideal for true dabblers and folks who love getting referral fees but aren't interested in really "doing real estate."

Whatever you choose, make sure it's in your budget. I'll remind you about that later.

Take a minute to check out what the office really looks like. Is the office clean, updated, easy to get to and find parking? Is the front desk staff pleasant and professionally dressed? If you were a client walking into the office, what would you think? The office and front desk staff are part of your image and reputation. Make sure what's being presented is a match for what you're all about.

CHAPTER 3

PROFESSIONAL IMAGE: SETTING YOUR OWN HIGH BAR

The bar to entry is low; set the bar high for yourself ... creating a professional image: communication, attire, passive communication, office environment, honesty, courtesy, accountability

Now that you've found a home for your license, think about your own professionalism. As we all know, in the United States, the bar is set very low to get a real estate license. To that end, how are you going to set the bar higher for yourself, so you outshine the competition and create a great reputation in your community and amongst your sphere and your colleagues?

Did you know that getting a real estate license in Holland is like getting a college degree? Their bar is set very high, for everyone, and it results in a field of higher-level professionals across the board. Other countries have no licensing or oversight at all, which creates the totally opposite professional environment. On which end of the spectrum do you want to be?

Here are some factors that go into creating a professional image:

1. Communication (quality, frequency, and response time);
2. Attire (your style is important);
3. Passive communication (email signatures and voicemail messages);
4. Office environment (convenient location, parking access, quality of receptionists, look and feel of the office entry);
5. Honesty, courtesy, and accountability.

COMMUNICATION – SAY WHAT YOU MEAN; MEAN WHAT YOU SAY

Good communication is the key to all successful relationships; just ask Dr. Phil. Real estate is founded on relationships of all kinds and they all require regular communication to stay happy-dappy.

When it comes to the quality of your communication, you have to consider it from multiple angles. For one thing, the quality of your communication means you are being clear, answering questions fully, using appropriate language (i.e., not being too casual, "taking a tone" with the recipient, or using curse words) and, when communicating in writing, using proper spelling and punctuation to the best of your ability.

you're	contraction of you are	You're welcome.
your	possessive	Is this your pencil?
their	possessive	I like their taste in music.
there	location	Let's sit over there.
they're	contraction of they are	They're meeting up at 6:00.

Learn it, love it, use it.

Since you can't really "hear" tone in a text or email, if you have a sensitive topic to cover, better to use the phone instead of sending an email that could be misconstrued. What to do when responding to a message when you're upset? Wait a few minutes, or a day, to calm down and collect your thoughts, so you're sure to respond professionally and not either regret your email or incite a verbal riot with the other party. If you really have to write them back, draft your email in a separate document first, review it, read it back to yourself a few times, choose diplomatic language, and make sure you're taking the high road and being the consummate professional before sending it off. You can only control your own words, not the other person's reaction, so be responsible for your communication.

Frequency is a big one, especially when you're cultivating a lead or in the middle of a transaction. You don't want a lead to go elsewhere because you haven't contacted them in some manner or other for months. Of course they could have called you when they were ready to buy or sell, but since they haven't heard from you in ages, they were vulnerable to being wooed by another agent in the meantime.

RING
RING
RING

Also, when you're in the middle of a deal and you or the other agent, or gods forbid the client, stop communicating and updating each other on what's happening, that's when the wheels fall off the bus and your deal can careen off the side of a cliff. Ahhhhhhh, crash!

There are so many deadlines in a real estate transaction; to list them all would take forever and be boring to read. Not to mention that they vary from state to state. Suffice it to say, there are a lot of deadlines to keep track of, and if you let one pass, you're out of contract, and the other party has a right to cancel the deal at no penalty to them, but at a penalty to your client, who just lost a house or a buyer. Ouch!

Let's say you have a deal where you represent the buyer. Inspections are taking longer than expected to complete, and you need more time to schedule another specialty inspection and get a response back to the seller. You'd better draft an addendum to your contract ASAP, have the buyer sign it, and get it over to the listing agent with an update on what's going on, so all parties are on the same page and your contract remains valid.

It really stings to have your client lose out on a house due to your professional shortcomings. That also smells like grounds for a complaint against you. To avoid that ugliness at all costs, create a system to track the deadlines and calendar reminders to yourself so you don't miss something. Even note deadlines the other side is supposed to meet. If you're of the mindset that you have to do the other agent's job in a deal, you will be more likely to have fewer problems and more successful closings, because you were on the ball.

I've even gotten property management business from someone who had bought a listing of ours years before. They'd had their own agent at the time but ended up with such a positive impression of our team that they reached out to us when they needed property management services. Didn't see that coming. That was a huge compliment I am continually grateful for.

Particularly if things are getting hairy, it behooves you to update folks frequently on what's happening so no one has space to freak out. Even if there's no new news, tell them that! That's something I see in the escrow world a lot. An escrow officer or assistant will ignore calls and emails from a buyer or seller because they have nothing to tell them. Newsflash: people still want to hear your voice, even if they aren't learning something new. It comforts them at a time when they are feeling unsure and anxious about their deal.

And now, response time. We live in a world that seems to be going faster and faster as the years go on and new-fandangled technology comes our way to put rockets on your roller skates. Wheeeeee!!!! Such toys are both a curse and a blessing. On the one hand, mobile devices and cloud computing allow you to be reached anywhere and work from anywhere. On the other, mobile devices and cloud computing allow you to be reached anywhere and work from anywhere. You have to learn what your professional boundaries are and defend them (more on that later), or else you'll be run into the ground with constant texts, calls, and emails where people expect you to respond immediately. That's not maintainable, realistic, or practical in the long run.

What is reasonable is that you respond to all messages within 24 hours of receipt. Of course if the subject matter is sensitive, you should not put off responses if you really are in a place to get back to someone, even if the response is just "Received, thank you. Will follow up in the morning." That tells the other person you at least have seen their message and lets them know when to expect a full response from you. Again, it comforts the other person and helps avoid a blowup.

The beauty of our technology is that you can set up automatic replies if you are not in a position to respond to people in a timely manner. I use that feature all the time in my email. I love it on days when I know I'm going to be running between back-to-back field appointments and not able to check my email frequently and respond quickly. It sets up an expectation and also provides someone with a response right away.

Same goes if you are going to be in a class or seminar all day, or even out of town. Gods forbid you take a vacation and actually unplug from the world to recharge yourself. Keep in mind that, when you do unplug, you need to be sure someone else you trust is managing your business. Whether that be your team, partner, or another agent in your office you respect and trust, the choice is totally up to you.

Your voicemail is another place to set up expectations about response times. Personally, I use my office phone for all business communication. Very few people have my cell phone number. I just heard you gasp and quirk an eyebrow. I know; I'm not the norm on this. At my office, our voicemails get emailed to us, so I'm able to pick up messages anywhere and respond accordingly or forward to a teammate to handle if appropriate.

Because I direct all calls through my office phone, I change my voicemail every day. Yes, every single day. I say the date, when I'll be out of the office, and when calls left after that time will be returned. To date, I've had very positive feedback from clients and colleagues when they hear that message. They also know I'm in the office every day and working! It's good to remind people you are in business and productive.

The more productive you get, the more managing your schedule will become critical. I need my day to have a particular flow to ensure I get everything done in a timely manner. To that end, I tend to have all field appointments (showing property and such) in the afternoon so I can have my mornings free to catch up on all emails and voicemails. That gives me a clean slate for the rest of the day. Being a "zero inbox" person, it sets my mind right when I can clear away everything in my inbox at the start of the day. It's the little achievements that keep me going. Plus, if the afternoon goes crazy with unexpected appointments, I won't be adding fuel to a dumpster fire, since everything from the morning is done. Woot!

When large companies, law firms, and corporate America give their employees a separate device for work use, I'd say there's something to be said for separating work from personal life as much as possible. When I'm in the middle of "off time," it rattles my brain to get the rare text from a client or agent that plunges me into work mode, when I should be in relaxy mode. Talk about slamming the brakes on a good time!

My way isn't The Way. I will never say that it is. If you love using your mobile device for everything, then rock on, baby.

ATTIRE: LOOK THE PART

How you dress and physically present yourself says a lot. Although we shouldn't, we humans make a snap judgment about a person the second we see them. Knowing that, think about what your attire and posture might say about you.

For example, what does Figure A say to you, versus Figure B? Who do you want handling the largest financial transaction of your life?

To be successful in this business and promote a professional image doesn't necessitate wearing a suit and tie every day. My dad does, of course, but that also fits his personal style and the expectations of his type of clients. Conversely, there's another highly productive and successful agent in my office who wears jeans, sneakers, a t-shirt, and a team-branded baseball cap every day. When he dresses up for something, we all notice and give him a good-natured hard time for being out of uniform. That works for him, though, and he works with folks who are very cool with how he dresses. He's also very professional and knows his stuff. I don't think you'd catch him showing property in his sweats, though. Even he has limits.

FIG. A   FIG. B

DON'T!   DO!

Your clients are your target audience. If you want to specialize in ranch sales, then jeans and quality cowboy boots are totally great and encouraged. Your attire allows you to relate to your clients, too. If you walk into someone's multi-million dollar home in clothes that are ill-fitted, torn, or inappropriate for the quality of the location, what level of professional will they think you are?

Side note for the gents: Make sure you are wearing the right size of shirt and pants. It's not a good look when your collared shirt is billowing around you, or spilling out of the back of your pants because it's too big, or your pants are hanging awkwardly low and piled on top of your shoes because they are too big and long. A well-cut suit is very striking and makes a phenomenal impression. You don't have to spend a fortune for one, either. Pick up a couple if you don't have one already. You'll be glad you made the investment.

Side note for the ladies: If what you're wearing to work could also easily double as a clubbing outfit, probs not a good choice. Also double-check that "the girls" aren't getting too much airtime.

In this day and age, if you have body modifications (piercings, tattoos, unnatural color in your hair), no one should be shocked by it. In fact, on some people, such modifications can be downright attractive, when done well. There's an agent I know who has beautiful, short, naturally white hair, and the bottom edge of her hair is dyed dark purple. It looks awesome! Same goes for tattoos and piercings. A lot of the time they look great, especially when the person is dressed well. The ground for that gets shaky when tattoos show up on someone's neck or hands. I don't think our society has accepted tattoos in those areas as professional yet.

I liken the rule to that of dining out: If the wait staff is dressed nicer than you, you are the one who is underdressed. As a rule of thumb, it's always better to be overdressed than underdressed. You are the professional; look the part.

PASSIVE COMMUNICATION: COMMUNICATING WITHOUT SAYING A WORD

Passive communication means anything you aren't directly sending to someone in the course of a conversation, such as your email signature, voicemail message, and out-of-office auto-replies. I've covered voicemail messages earlier, so let me just emphasize here that you should have a professional message that you change every day and that is short, courteous, and informative. If you decide to use just your cell phone and don't want to change the message every day, consider having a slightly longer static message that goes something like, "You've reached the voicemail of [say your name]. My business hours are Monday through Friday from 8 a.m. to 5 p.m., and I am available by advance appointment only on Saturday [or whatever your designated business hours are]. Please leave me a detailed message, with your phone number, and I will return your call at my first opportunity. Thank you."

One of my pet peeves is a voicemail message that says, "I'm either on the other line or away from my desk." No duh! I don't need to hear that. The point is, you're not answering the phone. Just a simple "I'm sorry to have missed your call," is totally fine. I don't need to know that you might be in the bathroom. You have a right to pee, take breaks, and talk to people on the other line. Just call me back when you're able.

Email signatures are another opportunity to project professionalism. Whatever email service you use, there's the option to build a signature that shows up every time you initiate, reply to, or forward an email. Your signature should always have your name, title, company name (in Nevada you have to put your brokerage name on everything you send out), address, and phone number.

Adding little extras like a photo of yourself (no selfies, please), links to your social media, website, or service organization website are great as well. Ride the line between having a bold, abundant signature block and a crowded eyesore.

Remember your mobile device has this feature as well. Be sure to add a short and sweet signature to emails sent from your device.

If you don't know how to make or add an email signature to any of your devices, ask for help!

When it comes to out-of-office auto-replies, I'm a fan of the advice from the Emily Post Institute, where they warn against messages like, "I'm currently out of the office until [X date]. All messages received while I'm gone will be deleted. Contact me upon my return on [Y date]." That's just rude.

Instead, think about leading with courtesy and professionalism. Let the sender know how long you'll be gone, if you'll be able to check and respond to messages, whom to contact in your absence, and when you will be responding to messages. That way, if the sender needs assistance right away, they know who to direct their message to, and if not, they can kick back and know you'll respond by the set date. That's especially helpful if you're going camping, leaving the country, or otherwise someplace where you don't have reception or the ability to respond at all. Remember, it's okay to unplug—just make sure you have a system arranged to cover your business while you're gone.

OFFICE ENVIRONMENT: SETTING THE MOOD

Since your front desk is always your front line for making a first impression when a client comes to your office, be sure it reflects your level of professionalism as much as possible. Unless you're the broker, you can't control how the staff talks or dresses, but if you've aligned yourself with a broker who reflects your professional values, that will all likely be in order.

You can control your own personal office. If it's a place you're able to bring clients, versus a cubicle, take a look at it from a client's perspective. Is it welcoming and set up for visitors? Is there tasteful art on the walls? Does it smell good? Is it well lit? I don't mean just bright. I mean, is the lighting abundant and comfortable? Don't be afraid to pick up a stylish desk lamp to warm up the space and add some flair.

Are there papers and files all over the place, or does everything have a home? If you're having to apologize for the clutter, get to KonMari-ing your office ASAP.

HONESTY, COURTESY, AND ACCOUNTABILITY

Honesty should be an easy one, but it slips more than anyone would like. I also see this as overpromising or putting words in someone's mouth, especially when that person isn't there to set the record straight.

When you overpromise something to a seller because you're really dying for their listing but aren't able to—or just don't—deliver on it, you aren't being honest with them. Salespeople can get so wrapped up in the desire to make a sale that they forget what they are about and what services they actually provide. Getting really comfortable with your listing and buyer presentations will help you stay calm, cool, and collected during such meetings and let you focus on the client, articulating your value and coming to an agreement.

Rarely does anyone want to walk away from a listing or a buyer lead, but sometimes you need to. If you have an abundance mindset, it's not as hard. If you have a scarcity mindset, you'll stick with the worst clients, get abused, and do things in a deal you normally wouldn't—like agree to a huge concession on your commission or pay for things in a deal that you aren't really responsible for.

Courtesy ties all of that together. Coming from a place of courtesy makes all your efforts and communications inherently more profes-sional and better received, because the other party feels cared for and respected. Some things we do in our business aren't required, but it is a courtesy to our clients and even to our colleagues and makes things work better. Gods forbid you have a reputation amongst other real estate professionals for being a courteous person and a pleasure to work with. Saints alive!

If real estate agents are to be respected as a whole and have a better reputation as professionals, they need to commit to a higher standard of excellence than what is average or "expected" in the industry today.

CHAPTER 4

CHOOSING A MENTOR

Finding a mentor ... you'll need a Yoda to talk things through when stuff gets weird ... do the right thing ... qualities of a good mentor ... listen to your Spidey-sense

When you're new, you oftentimes are entering the business alone. Occasionally a new licensee is joining an established team as a buyer's agent, or joining an established family practice, and there's more structure that offers guidance to the new recruit. But how are you supposed to really learn the business when you're solo?

Find a mentor! Sometimes that's easier said than done. When your broker randomly assigns one to you, as was done for my mom when she got her real estate license, you have no idea how good that agent is and if they are teaching you bad habits or a bad way of doing business.

Since you followed the advice from the last chapter, you clearly have an awesome broker, so that person at the very least will be a solid guiding light for you.

I'm grateful that my dad was my mentor. He taught me a more sophisticated way to approach everything. It made me a better agent right out of the gate and created a sound foundation for me to build from and learn and develop my own style. Remember, I'm the outgoing one and he's the reserved, analytical one. Needless to say, our business styles in practice are very different but complementary. Like chocolate and peanut butter.

This book is designed to give you a solid foundation from which to operate, but you'll need a Yoda to help you along the way when stuff gets plain weird. What do you do when a deal is going sideways, and people are getting upset and Hulking out? What do you do when you think a client is asking you to do something unethical or illegal but you're not really sure of the statute or the precedent, or even what to say so you don't make things worse? What do you do if you see another agent engage in such behavior? What do you do when you have an issue with a contract and aren't really sure how to proceed?

These are examples of just some of the things you'll encounter. You'll want a trusted source to take your issues to and help you work out a good solution.

If no one is around in a moment of need, here's a little device to keep in the back of your mind when considering what to do or say next: When explaining—in your mind, in your imaginary future—what you did or said, start with, "Yes, Your Honor, I...." If what comes after that would make you cringe to say it in front of a judge, DON'T DO IT! Depending on what is happening in your deal, you may find yourself defending your actions to an authority figure, be it your broker, your Real Estate Commission or Board, or even, yes, a judge or mediator. I love the expression, "Do It Right. Do the Right Thing." It's such a great guide when you're caught in a stinky, festering mire of a situation. Always being able to step back and say, with confidence, that you did the right thing and remained professional is huge.

This is a relationship business and, depending on the size of your market, you are very likely to bump into clients around town and have other deals with the same agents. Even though not every deal ends well, or even successfully closes escrow, you can always do your best to remain the consummate professional, which lets you hold your head high and approach those future interactions with no shame or fear.

Don't be the agent everyone else dreads working with because you act like a pouty toddler when things get a little rough. Put on your big-kid pants, check your ego at the door, and focus on what's really going on and what you can do to fix it.

I am very grateful to work in an office where I feel comfortable asking any other agent for advice or their perspective on something. Sometimes, even just voicing the issue out loud can help open your eyes to a solution, or release all the anger you were previously feeling.

TEACHABLE MOMENT: Your mind is a dangerous place to walk alone.

In the isolation of our own heads, all our fears, frustrations, and annoyances seem totally valid and warranted. When we speak things aloud to a disinterested third party, we oftentimes see those complaints for what they really are—silly distractions. Shake that off and get focused.

Do you have a friend who always seems to have a good answer to your questions, especially when you're carrying a lot of emotion around an issue? Do they respond with a calm, considerate perspective that pulls you back from the ledge of self-righteousness and blaming others? Keep that friend close and let them be your Obi-Wan when your internal dialogue is having a field day playing Darth Sidious. Don't listen to that guy; he's the worst.

Since you'll be approaching your entry into the real estate industry with a business mindset and a commitment to ethics and professionalism, your "Spidey-sense" will tingle when your assigned mentor is dishing out crazy talk. Listen to your gut and feel the Force. It's all around you and won't lead you astray.

Part the Third: The Rock (bedrock, that is)

Chapter 5

CHOOSING A BUSINESS MODEL

What kind of business do you want? ... pinpoint your geographical market ... choices: buyers/sellers, luxury/everything else, ranches/suburban, commercial/residential ... relevant professional designations ... your professional boundaries

You have a real estate license; you've picked a stellar brokerage; you have a Yoda. Now, it's time to choose a business model. Remember, you want to be successful in this business and have longevity. Well, now it's time to create a foundation for that. Even if you are a hobbyist, but want to be sure your hobby is reasonably consistent and productive, you still need to think about this stuff and put it into action.

Let's imagine a ladder where the bottom rung is where you are operating solo and involved in every aspect of your business. We'll call that rung "busy." Next is a rung where you are solely focused on dollar-productive activities and you are still handling a little bit of admin work. Then comes a rung where you are only concerned with dollar-productive activities, like writing and negotiating offers, and have now been able to delegate all administrative tasks. After that, there's a rung where you are strictly focused on where you are at your highest and best use within your business, let's say two to three activities specifically. Up from that is a rung where you're only engaged in the business activity, or activities, you enjoy the most; you have a team handling everything else.

The top two rungs are two different approaches to retirement, or an exit strategy, that have long-term return to you as the owner:

1. having created such an efficient and effective system that you are able to be away a lot, enjoying the finer things in life;

2. or you can pick up said money-making machine and either move anywhere in the country, set up shop, and know you'll be successful, or branch out on your own, create a franchise, and take over the world. #goals

Whichever rung of the ladder speaks to you is fantastic. Choose powerfully and with intent. Achievement of the higher rungs of the ladder can look a lot of different ways. It doesn't mean you have to create a huge team of buyer's agents to push you to the top or have a team of five assistants under you. It all depends on what you're going for and what success looks like to you.

If you like to travel a lot but you also love coming back and getting right back into the mix of your real estate business, perhaps being at a level where you can engage in the activities you enjoy the most is a great fit for you. Building a team will get you there, and it can be as small as two other people.

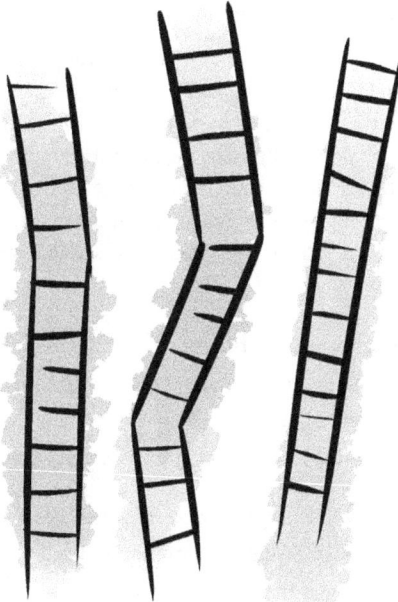

Thinking of those rungs, here's an approximate layout of the personnel combos you could have:

- Rung 1 - Just you, the lone wolf;
- Rung 2 - You and a part-time assistant or in-house transaction coordinator;
- Rung 3 - You and a full-time assistant;
- Rung 4 - You, another licensee who can work with buyers and sellers, and a full-time assistant;

- Rung 5 - You, another licensee who can work with buyers and sellers, a full-time listing coordinator, and a full-time escrow coordinator;

- Rung 6 - You, another licensee who handles nearly all buyers and sellers (they have taken a team lead role), a full-time listing coordinator, a full-time escrow coordinator, and a runner (runners are great for things like placing and removing signs and lockboxes, plus tending to other office errands so everyone can stay focused on higher-value tasks);

- Rung 7 - take your team you created for Rung 6 and run with it! You can take everything you've created in rung 6 and replicate it to either open your own brokerage and create multiple locations or personally relocate to another market and set up shop there, train a team, retain some level of ownership, and keep going. You can essentially become your own franchise, because you have replicable and scalable systems and procedures.

There may be more than seven rungs for you. Some other positions to consider are: marketing coordinator, buyer's agent(s), technology coordinator (IT services), general administrative or office assistant, personal assistant, inside sales agent, and even a stager for your listings.

It gets more expensive the larger your team gets. Take some time to think about what it is you want to create for yourself and others. If your mouth is watering at the prospect of a large team, just because of the money it could bring to you, back that truck up. A team is a team. They are not there to make you rich. Your team has goals and desires as well. The structure should operate to help everyone on the team achieve their goals. The more deals you close as a team, the more money everyone makes.

Do you want to add a property management division to help create consistent income to either help cover your overhead, or create a base salary for you while you're getting started in sales?

If you're stoked about a Rung 1-3 model, it'll be super important that you focus on organization and systems (they are important no matter what, but especially when you are directly responsible for executing nearly every task within your business). Even if you end up wanting to test out a higher rung, the whole thing will be built on the foundation of your systems and structures. At Rung 1, you're doing every job and task, every day. I think that's awesome because you'll have a true understanding and respect for each cog in the machine. That'll come in handy when you hire your first assistant.

I'll get more into structures and systems later. For now, chew on these potential paths you could take and decide which one speaks to you.

A LITTLE FROM COLUMN A *and* A LITTLE FROM COLUMN B

Another part of choosing a business model is the type of clients you'd like to work with. Are you interested in selling huge ranches, mobile homes, standard single-family homes, luxury homes, vacation homes, or would you rather screw all that residential nonsense and defect over to commercial real estate, baby!?

Each comes with its own unique challenges and skillset. Once you've decided, you don't have to stay there forever, but it's best not to jump around all over the place, or else you risk knowing only a little bit about a lot, not providing the best service you could, and being spread way too thin professionally and geographically.

The beauty of picking a niche is that you can drill down and become an expert. It feels amazing to know a ton about your chosen market segment, be on top of trends, and be a source for clients and the community to get accurate info and advice. That comes from defining your lane, staying in it, and rocking its little socks off like it's your job. 'Cause it is.

In my market, for example, there are agents who not only do business in the Reno/Sparks area, but are also traveling to Fernley, Carson City, Minden, Gardnerville, Dayton, and Incline Village. Check it out on Google maps real fast. It's okay, I'll wait...

It may not look far apart, especially to those in large metropolitan areas like LA, but here in the Biggest Little City, we're spoiled when it comes to commuting times. We complain when it takes 30 minutes to get from one place to another. That's half of what a lot of people commute to work in a day, one way.

Suffice it to say, I believe there is abundant business to be had within my community and do not venture outside of that. I also love knowing other talented agents in those outlying communities to whom I can refer clients. Referral fees are real, y'all. Some licensees only do referrals and barely work with clients themselves. They still get a nice chunk of the pie when a deal closes. Not a bad system.

What is your market like? How much driving do you want to be doing? Are you able to concentrate your efforts within a narrower radius, or do you live in a more rural setting where everything is spread out? Cities like Tucson, Arizona, are good examples of a big city that's really spread out but offers a plethora of business within smaller circles. With no cross-town freeway, I can see the allure in choosing to stick within just one quadrant of the city. That's a lot of stoplights in your day!

Salespeople have a tendency to want to please everyone and be all things to all people. That's not only impossible and unrealistic, it's also really destructive to you as a person. Every client thinks they are our only client, and when you're new, for your first few deals, that might be true, but it won't be true for long. How do you give that high level of personal service and attention when 50 people are pulling at you? (This is why self-care is real and should not be overlooked. More on that later.)

When you decide what kind of clients you want to work with and what kinds of property you want to sell, research what designations are out there that support this chosen demographic. Although "alphabet soup" behind someone's name can be meaningless when they have a dozen designations, being able to feature one or two that are directly related to the people you serve is awesome. It also shows you've gone the extra mile to get more, and better, education about that specialty than the average agent. Awww, you're so professional. I'm proud of you.

CHAPTER 6

PROFESSIONAL
BOUNDARIES

*Making room for your life ...defining your availability ... leveraging
technology to reinforce boundaries ... handling difficult clients ...
when and how to walk away ... listening to your gut feeling*

The last piece of the puzzle is figuring out your professional boundaries. I've already talked about the dangers of running your business through your mobile device and how consumers' expectations of response times and agent availability are insane. You're still a human being with a life outside of work. You need to be able to set up boundaries that allow you the time to unplug and also just do simple things like hang out with your family or go to the movies.

Setting up business hours, and making them known to your clients, is a great start. If we, as agents, want to be treated with more respect from consumers as a whole, we have to set proper expectations across the board. For me, it's a turnoff when a loan officer who's trying to get my business says, "You can reach me anytime. Ten o'clock at night, just call, I'll answer!" Wow, no thank you. I will be asleep at that hour, and you should be, too.

That being said, if you're a night owl and you do your best work after 7:00 p.m., I get it. Set up structures that allow for that, knowing everyone else is "off the clock." Perhaps that's when you enter your new listings into MLS, update your files and notes, draft market reports, or work on marketing projects.

A great agent I know is not a morning person, by a long shot. As such, he doesn't schedule any appointments before 10:00 am. There's another perk of real estate: you largely set your own schedule.

Just keep in mind that, whether you're a night owl or a lark, the person you've emailed or called may be the opposite, so don't expect an immediate response. Continuous caveat: if you have a crazy deal happening and people are on edge, or you've been trying to reach a client to schedule a meeting or new clients you need to nail down for an appointment, you're going to correspond at an hour you may not otherwise.

I mentioned earlier a sample script for your voicemail on your cell phone if you don't use two separate lines, that informs all callers of your business hours. The same can be done on your business Facebook page, website, and general office line. (This is especially helpful for teams. This way each team member can have individual voicemail messages, but the "main line" can have a static message with business hours, etc.) If you're a solo agent or partnership, consider the office front desk voicemail as the "main line." It should contain all the same awesome office-hour info. Leverage technology to set and reinforce boundaries and expectations.

Same goes for office closures. It's okay to be "closed" for holidays. Gods forbid you go camping in the summer or don't want to be bothered over major holidays like Yom Kippur, Christmas or Thanksgiving. Use your email signature to alert folks in advance that you'll be out of the office for a set time. That way they are mentally prepared when you are gone, and your out-of-office auto-reply will give them a contact to speak to in your absence.

Another type of professional boundary is how you handle abusive or unpleasant clients. You're not going to be a perfect fit for everyone you meet. Are you willing to fire a client if they are rude and disrespectful to you? If you're hungry for a paycheck, you'll probably put up with just about anything, but will it have really been worth it? After a few of those, your opinion might change.

Are you willing to walk away from a potential listing when you see red flags going up left and right during your initial meeting with a new client? If you are planning on staying in real estate for a long time, that kind of stuff will wear you down. It's best to practice walking away from a-holes now, so you can set a positive precedent for the clients you work with, rather than falling prey to your old habits of taking one on the chin and collecting your commission check with your head hanging low, promising yourself you won't do that again, but knowing you will.

That got dark. But it's something you need to think seriously about, preferably before the situation comes up. And it will come up.

Your broker may not cover that in training but should always be able to offer diplomatic wording to you upon request.

There are nice ways to not take a client on in the first place. You can say something diplomatic like, "It looks to me that we are not a good match to have a successful business relationship. I wish you the best with the sale of your home and thank you for your time." [Exit stage left.]

If you're already working with a client and things are not going well, you can say something like, "Based on experiences to date, I am not the best fit for you, and I suggest you secure a relationship with another agent," or, "This business relationship is no longer workable, and I will be giving you back your listing." [Send cancellation/withdraw instructions.]

Sometimes it may just be a gut feeling. Maybe a buyer you thought you could work with starts to treat you unprofessionally or without respect. Perhaps you even start to feel unsafe. Something about them begins to make you feel uncomfortable; something doesn't feel right. You can simply let them know that you feel that you are not the right agent for their needs and that it would be a disservice to them for you to continue representing them, and then refer them to another agent.

It just comes down to having a professional dialogue ready at hand and sticking to your guns when you know something isn't going well and it's not worth the abuse. Clients like that can also be a liability hazard: they are the ones who are quick to file complaints and lawsuits, or generally badmouth an agent without considering how their behavior led to their home not selling, etc. Nobody needs that in their life.

The intention of this book and my podcast is to help elevate your game, so our chosen profession can be respected across all communities and have that be reflected in receiving more respect from the public. The more ubiquitous higher standards become, the more things will change.

My hope for you is that you have a phenomenal real estate career and experience, and that the nuggets I share with you can help you avoid the pitfalls your predecessors whacked themselves on.

CHAPTER 7

CREATING A BUSINESS PLAN

Foundational Ideology, Strategic Plan, and Budget

*The Book ... personal standards of practice ... business plan ...
core ideology ... mission, inspiration, culture, beliefs, expectations,
strategic planning, funnels of business, lead generation ...
budgeting, tracking, and data ... office overhead, commission
splits, and referral fees ... CPAs and attorneys ... business entity*

Next stop on your adventure: create a business plan, a strategic plan, and a budget. The end result should be a big ol' book that sets the course for your business and is the foundation from which you operate. It will set a standard of practice for how you do business. Consistency is crucial to success. Knowing who you are as a small business will be your rock throughout your career and help you differentiate yourself from the competition, when you know what you stand for.

Your business plan is the cornerstone document that outlines the structure of your business. It's the skeleton you'll build on as you go. The first consideration is your foundational ideology. What is your purpose as an agent? Why are you in business? Even if you're planning on being solo, or only having one assistant for the foreseeable future, you still need to know and be able to express what you're about.

FOUNDATIONAL IDEOLOGY: YOUR BUSINESS'S BASE

Ideology is made up of a few things: your mission, inspiration, culture, beliefs, and expectations. You will approach every client, agent, and transaction from your ideology. Whether you're a solo agent or a team, having a foundational ideology is critical to a successful business. Corporate culture is a real thing, and when you think of Amazon, Starbucks, Coca-Cola, Walmart, Uber, or Hobby Lobby, a feeling comes to mind. Some corporations you'd love to buy products from or even work for, and others you wouldn't. A large part of that is the culture the corporations have and portray.

Culture can make or break a company. Culture can attract fantastic talent and boost your profitability. Most agents never think about the what, why, and how of their practice. They just walk into the business and stumble around in the dark. You are already light-years ahead of such agents because you are thinking about it and will be more noticeable in your market.

Get a writing surface and utensil. Now, write *Mission* at the top of the page. Brainstorm on the page what you're doing in real estate. The mission is your purpose (e.g., to be successful)—what got you into the business in the first place. It's okay if your mission is related to making money; that fuels your passions in life. This is America, after all, and you're not joining the Peace Corps.

Noodle that around until you hit on a statement that rings true for you. Remember, you aren't publishing this, so don't be embarrassed or shy about what you come up with (e.g., I'm in real estate to be profitable).

Next, write *Inspiration* at the top of another page. This is where you'll brainstorm on why you want to help people buy and sell homes. This is the inspirational statement that will excite you every day and help you focus when things are rough. It's also what attracts people to your team and gives them the motivation to see their tasks through each day, instead of seeing their role as just a "job" and feeling like it's a chore. Posting your inspiration statement in the office is a great way to stay present to the feeling you've created through it.

Mission and inspiration statements don't need to be long paragraphs. You're trying to express an idea clearly and concisely. It's okay if you start out with a bit of a novel; just keep tooling it around and refining it. After a few tries, you'll be able to distill it down to the core ideas.

Culture might be my favorite part. Write *Culture* at the top of the next page and jot down all the values you have as a person and as a professional. You know that old expression, "If you don't stand for anything, you'll fall for everything"? Well, having a clear and relevant culture will keep that from happening and help to shape and define your business identity. It keeps you on the straight and narrow, too, when clients and deals get hinky.

What do you stand for, and what do you want your business to stand for? For me, words like honesty, trust, teamwork, service, integrity, and proactive, which your future employees and teammates should hold as well. If you have someone on your bus who doesn't value honesty, holy Lord—pull over and kick them off.

Again, you don't need a list of 100 things, but 5-10 is reasonable. Don't hold back on the brain dump, though. Review your list and see which words are related and which words really ring as critical to you. If you were going to a desert island and could only take five culture characteristics with you, what would they be?

Next up, beliefs! Write that down. Your behavior is shaped by your beliefs and your behavior manifests in the actions you take every day with your clients, teammates, and fellow agents. Other people directly experience your beliefs when they work with you.

Do you believe in doing things right, doing the right thing, empowering yourself and others, trust, confidence, reliance, respect? Look to how you treat other people regularly and how others would describe you. Be honest with yourself if there's a soft spot in your behavior now, so you can address that in your culture and commit to beliefs that will build an iron Band-Aid over that weak spot and make you a better human and professional.

The last brick of your foundation is expectation. Dedicate a new sheet to that. This is your accountability buddy and how you follow through on everything you've just created. If you expect others to be on time, you have to hold punctuality as an expectation for yourself. Big-ticket expectations everyone should have: communication and follow through. Leads and deals are lost due to lack of consistent and clear communication. The same can be said for follow-through. Do what you say you're going to do, when you say you're going to do it.

Whatever you expect of yourself, you should expect of anyone who comes to work with or for you. If you have someone in your professional orbit who does not share what you are now creating, you will have huge clashes and it won't be pretty. As a preview to the info I'll share about hiring: hire slowly, fire quickly.

Here are some ideas for you to kick around while you're writing down your list of professional expectations: follow through, ask questions, communicate, be creative, be your best.

Once you're happy with everything you've written down and have the distilled versions of each section (mission, goals, culture, beliefs, and expectations), put it into a well-laid-out document and print it out. Call it something cool and be proud of it. Don't let it get dusty in a drawer and forget all this great stuff you made. It'll be nice to have it handy and use it as an onboarding manual for new employees. They should get a copy, too, and be familiar with the contents.

STRATEGIC PLAN: THE HOW OF GETTING BUSINESS DONE

Strategic planning is the "how" of your business plan. You've just laid a beautiful foundation in the previous exercise, and now you need a plan of attack to achieve your productivity goals.

Being new, you may not know what is reasonable to expect to achieve in your first year. Don't worry about it. Number one, everyone is different. And number two, there is no "should" or set standard of productivity for a noob or anyone else, for that matter. Instead, think about how you define success, what amount of money you need to cover your bills (we'll get into budgeting next), and what amount of money will help you achieve your personal and professional goals (e.g., taking vacations, growing a team, or planning for retirement).

Do a bit of research to get clear on the average sales price in your market, and for your chosen market segment. Check out commission offerings and make a decision on what you will charge for your services. Take a look at market times to understand how long it takes the average listing to sell, and make a reasonable guess as to how long it takes a buyer to find a home, make an acceptable offer, and then close escrow. That will tell you how long it will take to get a paycheck, and thus, how many deals in a year you need to do to meet your goal.

If you're starting out knowing no one and have to build your sphere of influence from scratch, be conservative on your estimates. If you blow them out of the water and do better than you planned, hooray! If you have a huge sphere that you can reach out to, you may want to push yourself a bit on your goals.

Perhaps your goal is to do five transactions this year. Super! Now do the math to multiply the average sales price by five and then multiply by the average commission and you've got your gross revenue. That alone can be a goal you set: gross commission earned per year.

If you decide to establish a team down the road, everyone should have input on the transaction goal (how many deals you do in a year), because everyone who brings in business should have an opportunity to earn a bonus when that business closes. Money is a fantastic motivator, and if you've set up a structure to compensate for such things, it'll be effortless and painless to implement, and sustainable enough to keep going for years.

Word your chosen revenue in the positive. Because what we think about we bring about, right? "My revenue is $xxx or more." Great! Write that down and post it where you'll see it every day.

Know that although real estate sells year-round (in most markets), there may be some months where activity goes down and other months where it goes up. Learn that about your marketplace, so you can divide up your transaction goal over the year in a reasonable way. So don't put a goal of five closings in January if your market is really slow, or nearly dead, at that time of year. If you live in a place where vacation homes are the primary commodity, then the off-season may be dead for real estate sales. That's totally okay; just plan for it.

Real estate is cyclical in a lot of ways, and optimal buying seasons is one of those ways. This is yet another reason why budgeting is so important. Make sure you squirrel away your acorns in the summer to make it through the winter, so to speak. If you work in a market where winter vacation homes are hot, then you may have an opposite squirreling season.

Being really clear on how much revenue you want to generate and how many deals it'll take to make that happen lets you get hyper-focused on your lead-generation activities and also gives you a clear target to aim for—and something to celebrate when you reach it.

If you love data, consider making a tracking system for how many lead-generation calls you make a day and see how many of those calls turned into appointments and how many appointments turned into clients and how many clients turned into closed deals. You can track everything from calls to notecards and personal meetings, to client parties, mailings, referrals received, and more.

Knowing where your business comes from will help you focus your efforts and dollars where you get the highest return. Why spend thousands of dollars on a lead-generation system or mailings that give you zero return, when all of your business is coming from open houses and participation in your local service organization?

When you're just starting out, you may not have a sense for your "funnels of business" yet, so try out just about everything. The one thing I would caution everyone on, whether you're new or not, is paid lead-generation systems like Mega Agent, Tiger Lead, etc. First off, they tend to be incredibly expensive (so can Zillow if you want to pay them for leads) and take a huge bite out of your budget. Second, they rarely pay for themselves over time. Third, and most frustrating of all, they don't actually deliver the "qualified leads" they promise.

By honing your craft and practicing dialogues, you will have more success at converting ad/sign call leads, people visiting an open house, or someone you chat with at an event, than you will with paid lead-generation services. It all comes down to your skills as the real estate professional, not a shiny, expensive feeding trough.

The bone I will throw is to lead services like HomeLight, Boomtown, and Referral Source. They only collect a referral fee at closing and don't charge an up-front fee. Isn't that always the red flag for scams on Craigslist—someone asking for a large sum up front? Not to say those other companies are scammers. Don't send me a nastygram.

Let your budget be a gatekeeper of your ability to pay out referral fees. If you're getting business that way, but always giving up 25%-35% of your paycheck on top of your broker split and operating costs and not bringing in enough of your own business, your cash flow will suffer.

Your strategic plan should be flexible, and you should review it at least twice a year to make sure it reflects what's really working in your business. If you get a wild hair and want to try out a new tactic in your business, go for it. Just add it to your plan so you can reflect on its effectiveness down the road. The strategic plan should be a living document and will reflect the evolution of your career and business. It should never get filed away and forgotten about. In business school, we were told that the most successful CEOs and business founders kept their business plans out on their desks as a reminder of their plans and commitments. Who knows if that was really true—but it sounds like good advice.

BUDGET: SHOW ME THE MONEY, BABY!

It's budget time!! Woot!! Break out your spreadsheets, y'all, 'cause we've got costs to track and formulas to make. Can't you just hear the rave music now? Where's your glow stick?

Your real estate business should fund your life. Your life should not fund your business. That's how burnout happens. You're too young for that. To that end, you must take your personal budget into consideration when making your business budget. It's all too easy to have one's personal budget getting fatter over time, as you achieve more success. Keep that financial waistline in check so you can maintain a savings account of six months' worth of living/personal expenses, or have a total freak-out when business has a prolonged slow spell or overall market value loss that materially affects your revenue. There are no financial sweatpants to expand into. You just end up eating away at your savings account.

Everyone's lifestyle is different; just make sure you're running efficiently at home, so as not to overburden your business. You can even budget for fun stuff, so it's not all gloom and doom. You should, in fact, have fun things in your budget so you can take the time you need to get away (even for a weekend) regularly and decompress, or even just have something fun to look forward to.

Compile a list of all your personal overhead [car payment, childcare, credit card payments, gas, groceries, health/beauty, insurance (home, auto, life), maintenance (home and auto), mortgage, travel, utilities, etc.] and fun expenses (going to the movies, buying new clothes, concert tickets, hobby stuff). Tally all that up in a spreadsheet and do your best to break all costs down by month, knowing some things are paid quarterly like a sewer bill or an HOA fee. Get in touch with that total and then set aside the figure of what a savings account balance would need to be to cover six months' worth of those expenses. Big number, right?

I found that tracking all my expenses and purchases on a spreadsheet did not work to help me save money or spend less. What it did do was show me where I wasted money and that I should have a bunch of money left over at the end of each month, instead of overdrawing my account so much. If you're also not a spreadsheet person, like me, I still vote that you do this exercise, just to see where your money is going. If needed, track all your receipts for 30 days to see where the holes are.

Leverage technology to your favor. I love an app called Daily Budget. After entering your net income and all your "must" expenses (e.g., mortgage, childcare, groceries—the stuff that if you didn't pay it, life would fall apart) and other life expenses (e.g., oil changes, club dues, Netflix subscription, savings goal, etc.), it then calculates everything down to the money earned and spent per day, and leaves you with what is really available to you to spend as you wish per day: a daily budget. Get it?

Using an app like that will keep you on track with your personal spending, so you can maintain a high level of integrity there and not have to leverage your business as a piggy bank to get you out of a pinch or help you pay for a new car or expensive vacation. Big no-no.

Going through this exercise will also give you the answer to how much money you need your business to make in order to pay you what you need to live. Again, this is why you should take a look at your lifestyle and make sure you're able to bring in what's needed to keep you comfortable within the first year or two, depending on your level of savings.

If you have other sources of income, like investments, income property, etc., keep track of those, too. Perhaps you will only consider additional/outside income as your savings source, or your rainy-day account. Just make sure you've accounted for it and it's part of your plan.

After your personal budget is dialed in, get cracking on your business budget. This should include things like advertising (for yourself and marketing of listings), bank fees, broker fees, software licensing fees, copies/printing, dues (board, MLS, designations), gifts (little tokens of appreciation to clients after a closing), health insurance, lockboxes, meals, postage, salaries, signs, supplies, telephone, coaching.

Please, please, please go over this with your CPA (whose fee should be in your business budget, too). There are a lot of different ways to track expenses and take deductions on your taxes. Make sure you're getting sound tax and legal advice from competent, experienced professionals. You don't need Uncle Sam knocking on your door because you did something naughty with your financial management.

A CPA and an attorney can help you decide which business entity (should you choose to use one) is best for you (LLC, S Corp. etc.). All of your options in this area have different tax and legal ramifications, hence don't shoot blind and start up an LLC because that's what your friend did, or what the internet told you to do, when another entity type is a better fit for your unique situation.

A CPA can also help you with all this stuff and either provide bookkeeping services, if that's not your strong suit, or recommend someone to you. It's super important to be sure you're tracking your expenses every month. How else will you know if you're staying on budget and maximizing your profit? I, for one, am not a spreadsheet person. The thought of managing QuickBooks and spreadsheets makes my brain itch. I'd rather spend my time engaging with people. Did I tell you already that I'm an extrovert?

If you love numbers and budgets, then you can save a buck and do this yourself. Just remember to schedule time each month to reconcile your accounts and make sure everything is ship-shape. Your future self who is dealing with end-of-year reporting and tax filing thanks you.

With all this shiny new data, you can fill in the holes of your revenue requirements or complete that exercise altogether.

The final piece of this puzzle is your long-term planning for retirement, or some other exit strategy. Remember, one of the risks of this business is that there is no one looking out for your retirement planning and polishing your gold watch. Work with a solid financial planner to help you get tools and products in place that will build wealth for you to enjoy in your precious retirement years, whenever those may be.

Selling successful real estate teams has become a thing. You are much more likely to get a handsome price for your team if it comes with effective and efficient systems and procedures as well as objective, historical data on productivity, lead conversion, and operating costs. If you don't have those, you're just selling your database of clients, which isn't worth as much.

Think back to your chosen business model. Is it just going to be you until you're done, or are you planning on creating a team and taking over the world? Either way, I commend you, and either way, your long-term planning needs to be considered.

You may need to adjust your personal and business budgets accordingly, once you have a plan in place. Again, this is a living document, like your strategic plan, and you should be reviewing your budget at least twice a year, if not every quarter, to make sure your train is on the right track. Knowing exactly what it costs to run your business and your life will help you make smart hiring decisions and be able to compensate your employees appropriately. This will also allow for reasonable transparency with your future employees, should you choose to have them.

The combination of the business plan, strategic plan, and budget is a bible from which to operate for the rest of your career. Too many agents never take the time to put these critical components on paper, let alone think about them, and their business suffers, or they are constantly in panic mode to get more business, and they think they aren't successful or the sky is falling. That's just because the cost of their lifestyle is squashing them, or they are not in touch with their overhead. Since you're brand new, get on the right foot now and reap the rewards later.

Chapter 8

SYSTEMS AND PROCEDURES

Develop systems and procedures manual ... every deal follows the same basic steps ... staying on top of purchase contract deadlines ... checklists ... client database ... desk/office setup ... How do you organize? ... routines for success

Now that you've written the most amazing foundational bible ever, why not make a systems and procedures manual?! Two sexy topics in a row, you say? Don't know if you're up to it? Buck up, baby!! This is the stuff that'll make you a lean, mean, money-making machine.

Knowing you're planning on being very productive and managing multiple transactions and clients at the same time, you'll need a system that works for you in order to ensure everything is done properly, on time, and consistently. Reinventing the wheel with each deal is nonsense. Don't do that.

> TEACHABLE MOMENT: A checklist is only good if used. If you're going to take the time to make one, use it.

There are plenty of transaction management and CRM (customer relationship management) systems out there, and I'm sure you could create your own for free, leveraging Google docs, Outlook task features, etc. Let's say, for the purposes of this lesson, that you are going to pony up for a system like TopProducer to track your leads, clients, and transactions. Great, congratulations.

TopProducer lets you build your own "activities lists," which is just another way to say checklist. It's where you can create a unique checklist for processing new listings, escrows, lead follow-up plans, long-term contact tickler reminders, and more. Although real estate is very dynamic and never boring, each deal must follow the same basic steps. Don't ever let the routine of these steps fool you. If you miss one, everything could blow up and it'll be your fault. Not a fun place to be.

Plus, a purchase contract has a ton of deadlines that need to be met, otherwise one party is out of contract and the other can cancel with no penalty to them if they don't like how things are going. Also an unpleasant situation to be in if it was your oversight that led to the deadline being missed and resulted in your client being out of a deal. Oops!

As you're learning new software and the procedure for activating a listing or processing a sale, write down each step (as painful and tedious as it may seem). I'm talking, make it so specific and step-by-step that a temp could come in for the day, sit down with this manual you've created, and get a listing activated. It may take that person all day, but it'll be done and it'll be done right. Update that manual as your procedures evolve or your technology changes. That way you never have to suffer the agony of a mass update five to ten years, or more, down the line when everything might be dramatically different. You're not going to want to do it then, so do it now while you have the time.

This brilliant manual will come in super handy when you bring on an assistant. Training will go so much faster when your new hire has this manual to walk them through the steps, while you explain the nuances of your business and how and why you do things the way you do.

The beauty of having an assistant is that they will be responsible for keeping the manual updated so it reflects new steps in your procedures. And you can make it a performance measure to review the manual each quarter to ensure it's up to date. Delegation, baby!!

These checklists and systems will also help you manage your weaknesses. We all have them; it's okay. I'm not great at long-term follow-up. I have to use calendar reminders and flags in our CRM to help me remember and stay on top of long-term communication. Gods bless calendar reminders!

Create a policy for how you title or categorize the people in your database. If you're getting involved with a system like Buffini right off the bat, you'll probably want to label clients as A+, A, B, C right away, so you don't have to go back and do it later. Whatever makes sense to you, make it a policy so future teammates or employees know how to categorize clients your way and your database stays consistent and makes sense.

Having steps on your checklist at the end of a transaction for long-term client follow-up is great. This way you won't forget to put that client on a plan to keep in touch and continue to develop that relationship and ask for business and hopefully get their referrals and future business the next time they need to buy or sell.

Keeping track of the strength of these relationships will also help you develop a "Top 100" list of the clients you work with the most and who refer you to their sphere the most. You may want to think about giving that group a bit more attention, since you know it'll result in income for you.

FILE OR PILE?

What kind of organizer are you? Are you a filer or a piler? Both are valid means of organization and both need to be done on purpose. What you want to avoid is just a scattered mess of papers, to-do lists, pens, and your lunch all over your desk.

Organization is the key to efficiency. Your systems and procedures are their own kind of organization. Your physical space, and even your digital space, affects your mindset and ability to focus. If you're always walking into a shit storm, you will likely always feel more stressed out or on edge, versus walking into an orderly space, where you'll feel calm and focused.

Step back and assess your office setup. Is your desk the right size and shape for what you need? Are you working from a tiny desk that barely has room for your computer, let alone a space to set files or review documents? Time to upgrade!

Although I love the look of sleek, modern desks that are basically a sheet of glass on shiny metal legs, they are incredibly impractical. Where do you file things? Where do you keep your gum?

Thinking of your office as the cockpit from where you "drive" your business, you want it to be functional and tailored to you, where nearly everything is at your fingertips. Especially in an era where everything is becoming paperless, you likely need more focus on your digital organization than on having ample storage for files and binders.

Make sure you're not having to walk across the room to get something you use all the time. It should be on, or in, your desk.

How's your lighting? Is it garish overhead lighting that buzzes? Is it way too dim and you're slowly losing your eyesight? Get a stylish lamp for your desk to help "set the mood" for productivity and also have something nice to look at in your space.

Did you know office chairs have a time rating? Are you spending six to eight hours a day in a three-hour chair? No wonder your butt hurts every day! Make an investment in a chair that is designed for your needs. As agents we do spend time in the field and don't have a traditional desk job. However, we do plenty of work in front of our computers when we're writing offers, running market reports, entering listings, updating our CRM, etc. Especially if you're a one-person show, you're spending more time in your chair. Might as well make that time as comfortable as possible.

Hate a traditional desk? Why not look into a standing desk, an adjustable-height desk, or a treadmill desk?!

In addition to your desk and chair game, think about your posture. All too often we end up in caveman mode, hunched over our computers like Smeagol over his Precious. Not a good look, and it's also really painful. When sitting in your chair, with proper posture, your monitor should be straight across from your gaze. You shouldn't be looking up, down, or sideways at your screen.

Adjust your keyboard accordingly as well, so you're not straining to reach it, or using T-Rex arms to type.

Get your organization dialed in from day one. If you see an inefficiency down the road, make an adjustment.

SUCCESSFUL ROUTINES = FLEXIBILITY

With very little warning, our schedules can go to crap. Right when we think we have this beautiful open day and plan on tackling a nagging task, BAM! we have clients coming out of the woodwork who want to see property, or snap inspections, or walk-in visits from clients to deal with. Well, there goes that open day you were looking forward to.

If you set up a good routine and adhere to it every day, you should be able to roll with such chaos fairly well. For me, that looks like addressing every email in my inbox and returning any calls first thing in the morning, plus updating my voicemail. That way, if the afternoon blows up, I can run out into the field with a clean slate and not feel overwhelmed with a lot of loose ends on my mind, plus whatever I'm heading out to deal with.

For this reason, I tend not to schedule any field appointments in the morning. I'm really protective of that time because I know what can happen. It's also nice to be able to accommodate a client quickly for an unexpected afternoon appointment and show up feeling focused and prepared, not distracted or overwhelmed with bending to meet the client while you are stressed about all the other stuff you dropped to make the appointment work.

Obviously you are going to do what works for you (remember, my way isn't The Way). If you prefer to address all email cleanup and phone calls in the late afternoon or evening, your routine will be opposite of what I do. As long as it works for you and you're getting everything done, clients feel cared for, and balls aren't being dropped, you're good.

If you're working from home, that is not a free pass to skip a shower and stay in your PJs all day. Didn't we just cover how appointments can pop up unexpectedly and you need to be ready to run out the door? Well, if you don't take the time to get ready for work, even if going to the office means walking down the hall, you're risking showing up for an appointment looking like hell, being late because you're scrambling to get presentable, or perhaps turning it down because there's no way you can get ready and be there on time. All of those are not good, and very much avoidable if you approach your workdays as such.

Get up, brush your teeth, shower, do all the things, and be ready to work.

CHAPTER 9

PERSONAL AND PROFESSIONAL DEVELOPMENT PLUS NETWORKING

Continuing education, relevant designations, the company you keep ... influences ... staying on top of industry trends, market values, and forecasting ... national vs. local market data ... farming ... head trash vs. a positive mindset ... budgeting for coaching, conventions, and seminars ... What does networking look like for you?

Let's tackle professional development first. If you're planning on having longevity in this business, you need to think about how you're going to stay informed about your industry and market. That can look a variety of ways and should include things like:

- getting relevant designations;
- attending high-quality continuing education and other classes;
- taking seminars to sharpen your listing presentation and home valuation skills;
- attending conventions or summits led by notable leaders in the real estate field;
- reading books that offer actionable information (like this one), not just books that get you pumped;
- hanging out with other successful people (regardless of industry);
- reading industry publications;
- attending forums and events in your city that provide information about what businesses are coming to your area and the overall economic forecast;
- listening to topical podcasts (like *Do It and Be Glad You Did*) that help keep professionalism, improvement, and evolution at the top of your mind;
- joining specialty associations to get in-depth education and tools to serve a specific group (NAGLREP, VAREP, NAHREP, and so on).

This list could keep going, but I think you get the point. If you are the sum of the five people you hang out with the most, your business is the sum of the five influences you allow into your brain the most (books, podcasts, classes, etc.) If you're new, you are in such a great place to make purposeful decisions about those influences right off the bat. If you've been in the biz for a few years and haven't really taken your influences into consideration, or taken them seriously, now is the time to do it.

All that being said, you also don't have to be that person who only ever reads self-help books and hangs on the word of every guru out there. That just creates a vicious cycle where you're always looking outside yourself for improvement and answers but never being in action. Instead, use the information you're gathering to reflect on, internalize, and see where and how you can apply what you're learning—and then apply it.

Success isn't "out there"; it's something you create. All the influences are awesome tools to leverage, and reminders to help you stay in action. If you want to split the log, you have to pick up the axe and swing. It won't be done by just thinking positive thoughts or only visualizing a split log.

Remember to have a generous sprinkling of fun influences in your life, too, so you have more to talk about than the latest self-help book you read. Variety is the spice of life, so shake it up and make something delicious!

Since books are cheaper than conventions and seminars, if you do prefer in-person learning opportunities, think about adding a line item to your budget to accommodate the cost of attending one, or two, or five, a year. It's all workable if you plan for it.

STAY IN THE KNOW

Staying on top of trends within the real estate industry is twofold: reading industry publications and websites (*Realtor, Residential Specialist, Inman News,* etc.), and paying attention to your market, chatting with other productive agents.

Reading industry publications helps you understand the national issues and trends that the market is experiencing as well as learn about new companies and technologies that may impact your business or the real estate industry as a whole (think e-brokerages and online offers through Zillow). We know that real estate is regional/hyper-local when it comes to values and cycles. The average consumer looks to national housing data to inform their opinion on what's happening in their area, but the two are not necessarily the same thing.

Thinking back to the market crash of 2008, some states were hit much harder than others. The market environment for the following five years also looked quite different in those states from markets elsewhere. Using national information can set an unrealistic expectation for the consumer, who may be unpleasantly surprised by what their local market is actually doing. They hear it's a seller's market everywhere, only to discover it isn't—or vice versa for a buyer…you get the picture.

If you're also in the loop on national info, you can counsel a client properly on how that data isn't relevant or applicable to your market and why. Being able to back up your perspective with local data is huge. If a buyer thinks the market is really low and they can get a steal, but your boots-on-the-ground experience and sales data shows otherwise, bring that to the table. Plenty of clients will still ignore you, but you've put it out there and can enjoy an I-told-you-so moment later. Although you'll never actually say "I told you so," because that's a dick move.

I have beef with our local real estate board because their market reports aren't an accurate reflection of our market, which you think wouldn't be the case, but we see it all the time. Because running a market valuation report is only as good as the data you use, and there's no set standard for what information is valid and appropriate (it's not a science), you can get very different pictures on the same market from any given agent or organization.

Farming—identifying a geographic area (neighborhood, subdivision, etc.) in which to focus all your marketing efforts to generate listings and buyers—is usually done with direct mail. However, with all the new-fandangled tech out there, you can also reach those people via social media ads. Scary internet spiders! If you are planning on leveraging farming as a lead-generation technique—something we will discuss in the next chapter—you have a great opportunity to dig deep, learn a ton about a select market segment, and use it to practice your pricing and valuation skills.

You can really get lost in your MLS system when playing with numbers and coming up with all kinds of reports. I think it's fun to run an evaluation on my own house to stay in touch with value, for my own edification, but also to understand what homes like that in general are selling for in the market.

You can use value reports to demonstrate all kinds of things. Keep in mind that if you're using the reports to make a point, make sure the person you're presenting the information to is a "numbers person." If they are, they'll surely see your point, and the report will facilitate the conversation. If they aren't, you may want to go with a colorful graph that displays the same information through a graphic, which will be more likely to catch and keep the client's attention and help you make your point. If you show a bunch of numbers on a spreadsheet to someone who isn't a numbers person, you'll lose them.

The combo of reading industry publications, real estate board market reports, and running your own reports is a great way to introduce you to your market and keep an eye on trends. You'll inevitably start to notice things after some time in the biz, and the more consistent business you do, the more you'll truly be in touch with what the market is doing. And that, my friend, is where you'll really start to develop your unique value as a real estate professional.

PERSONAL DEVELOPMENT, STEP ONE: CONQUER YOUR INNER DEMONS AND THRIVE

So head trash is real, and we all need to keep it in check, every day. There are lots of different names for head trash: negative self-talk, inner critique, mind goblins, The Saboteur. Whatever you call it, it takes real effort, in every moment, to keep in check.

We're not mindful or in control of our thoughts most of the time. If you see someone walking down the street and you have uncharitable thoughts about them, that's your head trash talking. If an exciting opportunity presents itself, and you're already telling yourself how the opportunity won't work out for you, or you walk into a room of new people telling yourself that no one in the room will like you, that's your head trash talking. It's super rude, and it's never on your side.

If you subscribed to the philosophy that "what you think about, you bring about," what would your thoughts be like? I bet they'd be awesome and they'd pump you up all the time. It'd be like having your own personal cheering section in your head. Woot! Get it! You rock! That feels way better, right?

When you're having a rough day, week, or month, what are you going to do to make sure you're keeping your thoughts out of the muck, focusing on solutions, and creating success for yourself? Remember, success isn't "out there" in the world, like some tasty treat someone hands you. It's "in here," in your mind, and you create it every day with your words.

Think back to the budget you made. Is there a line item for a coach, regular attendance at personal effectiveness training, conventions, and/or seminars that are all designed to help you with mindfulness and focus? The most successful people in the world surround themselves with amazing people, books, education, and experiences that keep them in a fabulous mindset. Now, I'm not saying you need to become some devotee of self-help gurus. You run the risk of matching tracksuits and alienating everyone around you.

It's about accountability on several levels: being held accountable for the thoughts you allow into your mind; being accountable for the words you let out of your mouth; being accountable to your clients, friends, and family; heck, being accountable to your personal goals. Most of us need a structure to help us follow through on all that. For some, it could be as simple as a 30-minute coaching call every two weeks. For others, it could be regular attendance at personal effectiveness classes, like Landmark.

Whatever it looks like for you is divine. Just make sure you figure out what works for you and stick with it. Make it a priority. I promise you'll be amazed at what you accomplish when you have a structure for accountability and mindfulness in place.

This business can be hard, and it weighs on people. It's another thing that leads to burnout. Right now that might seem dramatic, or you're thinking it won't happen to you, because, well, you're you, I guess. When you're dealing with an abusive client and/or a deal that is going all kinds of sideways, it's too easy to take things really personally and be emotionally invested. It's what leads to nasty emails you shouldn't send, or curt words you shouldn't say. It's also what can lead to really awful things like legal action or real estate board complaints. You're more likely to avoid those cesspools of poo if you have the mental tools at your disposal to deal with tense situations and difficult people. Really, those are skills you need in everyday life, so all the training and coaching won't be for naught.

Something to watch out for is getting stuck in a loop of inspiration and never being in action. We've all been there. You go to a convention or seminar and the speaker is amazing and their stories are engaging and you leave feeling pumped. Woot! You're smiling for hours and feel like you can accomplish anything. But as the days go by, that vigor you felt when you walked out of the event has waned dramatically and you haven't put any of your brilliant ideas into action and you're back to being frustrated with the way things are instead of creating what you want.

> **TEACHABLE MOMENT:** Inspiration is meaningless if it doesn't lead to action.

All the more reason to be sure you're sprinkling in motivational books and such with fun stuff that fuels you. Life is fun, and you can be a badass who gets things done. It also makes you more fun to talk to if you have exciting professional stuff going on as well as a full personal life. It's a harmony, after all.

WORK IT, BABY

Let's talk about networking. Let's talk about you and me. Let's talk about all the good and all the bad things that can be. Let's talk about networking.

I'm not the biggest fan of networking. Gasp! For as outgoing as I am, I get very nervous and self-conscious at networking events. It's because of my head trash, of course. See, I'm human, too. I still go to some networking events or business open houses to mingle and such, but I have found being involved in Rotary to be a much more comfortable place for me to share what I do for a living and then be open and available to friends in the club who ask me questions and want to work with me.

I see a lot of card-slinging at networking events, where it seems like everyone is just trying to get their business card into as many hands as possible. In a relationship business, can you really expect to get business from someone when all you did was shove a card into their hand, tell them your name and what you do, tell them to give you a call if they want to do something, and then walk away? What kind of impression does that make? They're more likely to toss the card out, or forget the person who gave it to them. Not a valid lead-generation tactic.

On the other hand, if you go to an event and talk to people, ask questions, and get to know them a bit, they are much more likely to remember you, have a positive impression of you, and consider using your services or referring you when presented with the opportunity.

Networking isn't just confined to specific business networking functions (those are the ones I'm not a fan of). It's also when you're at a birthday party for one of your kid's classmates or attending a community social function. There's a private social club in Reno called The Prospectors' Club. Members pay an annual fee, and the club throws awesome, purely social parties and events every quarter for the members. It's a blast. It's also a great way to meet people in a relaxed atmosphere, get to know them, and make connections with people that may become future clients or referral sources. I think the key to remember is that networking, in general, is just another way to plant a seed. It'll take time for it to sprout, so be patient and don't push people.

Another funny part about networking is that, although it's an opportunity to make business connections and expand your network, one's occupation does not define them, and sometimes people don't want to talk about what they do right off the bat. Keep some other icebreaker dialogues in your back pocket. Instead of saying, "What do you do?" you can say, "What's keeping you busy these days?" or ask about their recent or upcoming travel. People love to talk about themselves, so ask questions.

Plus, if the person you've just met is between jobs and isn't feeling great about that, it gives them an opportunity to tell you about a hobby they love instead, or perhaps travel or other goings-on that can fill the conversation and avoid a potentially touchy subject.

The art of conversation is just that. The more you can learn to be graceful in the dance, the more you'll connect with people, give a great impression of yourself, and make great connections that will boost your image and business.

CHAPTER 10

PROSPECTING

*Client attraction and retention ... your sphere of influence ...
funnels for leads ... farming, open houses, drip campaigns ...
lead-generation tools ... transactional or relational? Know thyself:
lead generation that fits your personality ... pop-bys, client parties,
notes, calls, silver bullets, inside sales agents, online leads, open
houses, billboards, radio ads, social media, targeted ads ... keeping
your marketing professional ... tracking and spreadsheets*

Now that you're ready to go fishing, what kind of bait are you going to use and how are you going to keep all the fish you catch? Not into fishing metaphors? Let's keep it simple. After all the work you've done to get licensed, join a stellar brokerage, and create a business plan, how you are going to generate and convert leads, and how are you going to retain the leads that have turned into clients?

The first thing you should mine is your sphere of influence. That includes your family, friends, past co-workers, and generally anyone that you know and see with some manner of frequency. Those are folks you can easily send a mailing to (thank you, Realtor stalking tools to find addresses!) announcing that you're now a Realtor and are in business. You can also leverage your social networking platforms to make the announcement and have a call to action that asks your sphere to contact you if they are thinking of buying or selling real estate, or know someone who is.

In the business planning chapter, I mentioned funnels for leads. Since you've decided what kind of properties you want to sell and what kind of clients you want to work with, you're primed to farm that demographic with targeted mailings or even Facebook ads.

If you're going to give farming a whirl, work with a marketing rep from a title company and they can help you create the farm and obtain the addresses you need for your mailings and/or a door-knocking plan. RESPA, which governs things like title companies, limits reps from what they can do for you, but at the very least they can give you resources to develop a farm, etc. Be sure to ask first if your request is RESPA compliant, so you don't put the title company in an awkward position.

Open houses are a way to get leads as well. Rarely does an open house actually sell the house, but an agent can often get buyer or seller leads from the folks who come through. This is another reason, aside from security, that it's important to have everyone register when they walk in the door. Try to collect as much information about your visitors as possible, so you can follow up after the open house and see if you've got a real lead on your hands. Don't be surprised or discouraged if you get a lot of neighbors or looky-loos coming to your event.

Have a loan officer at the open house, too.

1. It's nice to have the company if traffic is slow.

2. It's an added level of service to have a loan professional who can answer loan questions on the spot.

3. It's an added level of security for you when you're otherwise in a house all by yourself (especially in a vacant house and especially for female agents).

Loan officers can also get leads from an open house, since most buyers who do go to open houses likely haven't seen a lender yet. The loan officer can put the buyer leads on their drip campaigns as well, so the lead is getting followed up by you and your loan officer, and between the two of you, you can work to keep the lead warm and alert the other when they've finally raised their hand and said they are ready to buy. You both win.

Speaking of drip campaigns: It's possible your CRM or even the lead tools offered by your brokerage have free/included canned drip campaigns that are automated and do the work of keeping you at top of mind for you (as in, you're the first person they think about when it comes to buying or selling homes). Score! One less thing to think about and manage yourself. Just remember to enter all leads into that system when you first get their info. Add calls and notecards on top of that for a more personal touch—or better yet, invest in an app that allows those who sign in to your open house to be auto-entered into a drip campaign.

There are a ton of lead-generation tools and techniques out there. The only one I am going to revisit my warning about is a paid lead-generation service. I'm not talking about things like HomeLight that only take a reasonable referral fee; that's fine. I'm talking about things like TigerLead or Mega Agent that have steep monthly fees and sometimes also a referral fee on top of that (if they've since changed their fee structure, kudos, try them out).

Just know now: there are no silver bullets in this business. No lead-generation service can guarantee quantity or quality of leads. All the work is still on you to convert whatever it is they send your way, and quite frankly, a majority of the time the leads they do give you aren't great. Why not just leverage your in-house tools and sharpen your lead-conversion skills?

Think about how you use the internet and how often you just casually peruse things, like window shopping. You might be curious to know a bit more info, but you're not really in the market for a new pair of $1,000 shoes.

After taking a bunch of lead calls, you'll get a sense for if the caller is serious or not—yet another sixth sense you'll develop during your tenure in real estate, much like having a sense for value or how big a house is and such.

Another important factor when choosing your lead-generation funnels/sources is what kind of person you are when it comes to client/customer interaction. Are you relational or transactional?

If you're relational, you should primarily focus on loving your database and mining it for repeat and referral business. If you're transactional, you should focus on consistent mailing campaigns and other outbound marketing tactics to generate new clients, since maintaining the clients you've worked with isn't as high of a priority.

It's awkward when you try to squeeze yourself into a shape that's not authentically you. Other people can tell, too. If you don't like schmoozing with people or shooting the breeze with past clients and catching up on their goings-on, don't. Focus your efforts instead on building a very efficient and effective lead-generation system that keeps new leads pumping. Not to say a transactional agent won't get referrals or repeat business, of course.

For this, you may want to consider signing up for affordable lead-generation services that funnel you leads, plus hooking up with whatever lead-distribution system your broker offers, targeting mailings to your selected farm, hosting open houses with gusto, and perhaps hiring an inside sales agent who can make cold calls for you all day long. To be clear, I'm suggesting the affordable lead-generation services out there that attract consumers on their own and then send you their info when the consumer has asked to be connected with an agent. It's just another line in the water that doesn't cost you an arm and a leg.

Side note: although effective, this can be an expensive way to generate business. If that's cool with you, then go for it. Just remember that your marketing budget will need to be beefed up to accommodate for extra postage, letterhead, printing costs, online ads, etc. You'll also want to factor in the referral fee to lead systems and bonuses, should you choose to pay those to your inside sales agent for any leads they cultivate that result in a closed escrow.

Even transactional people need a system to keep in touch with past clients. You may not choose to invest in a client party or get together for drinks or a meal, but even just having them on your monthly e-newsletter or making sure they follow your business pages on social media is fine. Why not do the minimum to encourage past clients to come back to you or refer you? That's free business!

For those of you who are relational, your efforts will be mostly focused on your database and sphere of influence. You'll want to create systems that yield client retention, both for repeat and referral business. That can look a variety of ways, of course, but one of the most leveraged paths is a combo of monthly mailings, handwritten notes, calls, pop-bys (a Brian Buffini word for delivering a small item of value to past and/or current clients), lunch or coffee dates, and client events.

The idea being, you need to connect with the people that know, like, and trust you in order to stay at top of mind for those folks, so they always think to use you when they, or someone they know, is looking to buy or sell real estate. The more you show your value as an agent and as "the source of the source" for great vendor referrals and other information, the more you'll be on speed dial for your database and sphere.

Whether you're relational or transactional, at least cover your bases of consistent, ongoing communication with your database. Using an e-newsletter is an easy way to tackle that. Also, having a professional social media platform (Facebook, Twitter, Instagram) is another great way to promote listings, local events, and information, helpful tips, etc. with a large audience all at once.

Be careful with social media. Your professional profile should reflect exactly that—professional information—even if the posts are about "fun stuff." It should never include photos of you drinking, partying, spouting opinions about the world, or saying anything negative about a client or another agent in your community (even if you're not using names). Keep it classy, y'all. Don't make me get the ruler!

You'd think I wouldn't have to put in a reminder like that, but the instances where these kinds of posts are out there for clients to see is alarming. This is why you can have a personal social media profile for all that kind of stuff. You can adjust the security settings so no one sees your posts unless they friend or follow you. If you know someone well enough that they'd want to connect with you on social media and get such updates, then you've allowed that permission.

Keep your professional marketing platforms professional.

THERE IS NO MAGIC PILL. IT'S JUST WORK

The last thing I'll leave you with here is a reminder of the critical truth that there are no silver bullets out there that will provide guaranteed, vetted, high-quality buyer and seller leads. They don't exist. Bigfoot will be found and exposed before a legitimate, reliable lead-generation platform will be created that is the answer to all our lead-generation prayers.

The marketing pitches are so great! The thought and technology that goes into some of these platforms is amazing. But even with all the fancy bells and whistles, they still don't provide the leads they say they will. There's something about an intermediary reaching out to folks that either puts the consumer on edge or has them just say yes to the rep in order to get them off the phone. That's not a qualified lead.

The other big issue is volume. Not of leads but of agents. You are not the only agent the lead service is trying to get an agreement with. They are two-timing you, more like ten-timing. Sad but true. You can sometimes get a contract that gives you all, or part, of a select zip code or territory (for a hefty fee), but that's as exclusive as it gets.

A lot of times, a single lead is being sent to a handful of agents, and whoever connects with the lead first wins. With that kind of system, it can also overwhelm the lead when they get calls and emails from a bunch of agents within minutes of each other and now they're stressed out and soured on almost everyone, and then all the agents lose out on the lead.

This is why having your own personal inside sales agent is so appealing. It's one person who is dedicated to managing all your marketing campaigns and following up on all leads, just for you. Of course, when you're just starting out, that's not likely to be in the budget. However, if you go into business with a spouse, perhaps that's something you can arrange between the two of you. If one person is great on the phone but doesn't care much for field work or face-to-face interactions with clients, they can rock the phone all day long and pump out leads that the other person can convert and close.

Spouse teams can be good that way, even if the spouse gets their license just to be a more well-rounded and supportive assistant. That's totally cool and it saves the business money. I know a great husband-and-wife team where the wife started out in an administrative capacity and then developed into a buyer's agent, while her husband focuses solely on taking listings. It grew organically, which is a beautiful thing. Same goes for another awesome spouse team where one is the lead agent and out there generating business and closing deals, while his husband brings his valuable tech knowledge to the table and manages all marketing campaigns and tech solutions. Bonus!

Be cautious when considering a new marketing or lead-generation tool. Brand awareness is hard to measure, but it's valuable. It may not directly link to leads generated, but if more consumers are aware of you and your brand, they are more likely to work with and/or recommend you, simply because they've heard of you.

It's like during election season, when you go to the polls but haven't really researched the local candidates, so you just vote for the names you recognize from the posters and billboards you've been inundated with for the last few months.

You can track leads generated and dollars spent. If you decide to buy ad space on a billboard that costs you $10,000, you'd better get $40,000 in commissions from that ad. This is why you should make a lead intake sheet that asks the standard question, "How did you hear about me?" Sometimes it'll be obvious, because they are calling in response to a sign they just saw or even a website that syndicates your listings, and they tell you that up front. Other times, they don't specify how they got your contact information, so it's good to ask.

You can only measure and improve what you track. Keeping a detailed spreadsheet of all your marketing programs and how many calls you get based on each program—plus knowing how much each of those things costs you—will help you better understand where your business comes from and which marketing programs are the most effective, so you can continue to invest intelligently into the tools that bring you the highest return.

If you're not getting anything from that billboard, even people telling you that they saw it, dump it. Same goes for all the other possible programs and tools you can use.

If you end up getting a ton of leads from doing stellar, well-promoted open houses, then, kid, rock those out.

Don't spread yourself too thin and try to leverage every marketing tool out there. It's a waste of your resources, both financially and personally. It's exhausting to keep on top of your programs, leads generated, dollars spent, and the effort it takes to convert the leads into clients and then into closed escrows. Do your best to focus on a few (two to three) funnels/lead-generation programs. You can always make adjustments; add something and drop something else. Nothing is carved in stone here. Just make sure you stick with what works, but be sure to give each program a fair shake. If you don't get any calls after sending one letter, that's not a sufficient amount of time, or number of impressions, to make a judgment call. After having taken so many classes about lead generation and creating your own inventory, I noticed that it always comes back to the basics: be proactive, follow up with leads regularly (don't give up after one call and one email), provide great service, stay in touch with your database.

If you get really cozy with those basics now and make yourself an expert at them, you will have an easier time in this business and avoid pipeline frustration or being wooed by the siren song of lead-generation sales reps. Just put wax in your ears, Odysseus, and keep rowing!

CHAPTER 11

YOUR TEAM AND NETWORK

*Little black book of vendors ... building an external team ... lenders,
escrow and title professionals, inspectors, financial advisors, accountants,
attorneys, contractors, landscapers, and other vendors ... getting
and making referrals ... building your internal team ... hiring*

When you're just getting off the ground, your little black book of preferred vendors will likely be empty. That's okay. Through the twists and turns of each deal you do, you'll encounter new vendors and new challenges. From day one, think of each vendor and professional you work with to make a deal happen as being part of your team. You all have to work together in order to get the transaction closed, so be cooperative and respectful. All too often, escrow officers, especially, are openly disrespected by agents and clients because they have no clue about the amount of work it takes an escrow unit to process and close a deal. They probably have the most labor-intensive and detail-oriented job of all. I tip my hat to every escrow professional out there.

To get started, go ask the top-producing agents in your office who they use for escrow services, home inspections, and lending. Also ask them why they like those vendors. If it's just because the vendor is a friend, maybe that's not the most solid and convincing referral. If they work with that vendor because of their professionalism, communication, etc., that sounds pretty great. Try out their vendors and see what you think. Remember that each vendor you work with ends up as a reflection on you, so make sure you're working with other people who demonstrate your expectations of professionalism in what they do.

If you get negative feedback about a vendor you recommended, more than once, you need to dump them and move on. Of course, if you're working with a client who seems to have a complaint about everything or is just really grumpy and rude to everyone, you may want to let that roll off, but be aware of hearing about shoddy work, rude behavior, or lack of communication or professionalism. Those are biggies and should not be overlooked.

There are a lot of escrow officers and title companies out there. Use each deal you do as an opportunity to experience a new company and officer and see how they work. How do they handle bumps in the road? How do they communicate? Do they support you and your clients? Are they proactive?

I enjoy attending signing appointments because I get to see how the escrow officer interacts with clients. If they just push paper in front of them and only read the title of the document, I'm not likely to want to use that escrow officer again. If they take the time to explain each document so the client is aware of what they are signing, I'm excited about that and appreciative of the care and time the escrow officer is taking to create an environment of professionalism, trust, and expertise.

For those of you on the East Coast, your closings are handled by closing attorneys, which looks quite different than what we do on the West Coast. Either way, make sure the companies that you do business with are at least as professional as you are.

Although escrow holders are a neutral third party, it doesn't mean they don't have valuable insight to offer through the escrow period. Sometimes we're presented with funky things to work out in a deal, and oftentimes, if you let the escrow officer know about it in real time, they can offer you some helpful suggestions on next steps. Because they see that sort of thing all the time, they can offer tips to help avoid title issues that prevent your deal from closing.

Get to know a title officer. They are a wealth of information and guidance. They see all kinds of crazy things and can point you in the right direction when doing research on a property for a client. They are also incredibly helpful when you're working with someone who wants to buy or sell within a trust, corporation, or LLC. In those situations you need to make sure the human that's signing all the documents is the right human. Otherwise your contract is worthless.

What happens if you are selling a property, owned by a married couple, and one of them dies in the middle of escrow and the surviving spouse isn't on title? What if you find something funky on the title report and don't understand it but you know it seems weird? It may affect your transaction and cost someone money to deal with it. People can get grumpy when you touch their money. Seriously, the weirdest stuff can happen in a deal and you need to be able to ask these questions of knowledgeable experts so you don't make an ugly or expensive mistake.

WHO ELSE IS ON THE BUS?

Your next teammate is the loan officer. They are reliant on leads and referrals, just like you. Having an excellent relationship with a stellar loan officer can be very beneficial to you, since you're both in a position to refer clients to the other. They can also help keep your buyer leads warm and engaged while they are getting their ducks in a row so they can buy.

Also, they are often able to co-host your open houses and answer loan questions on the spot to folks who walk in the door. Remember, you are not a loan officer and should not be answering such questions, even if you know the answer. That's practicing outside of your scope, and it's always a no-no.

TEACHABLE MOMENT: Be the source of the source. That means be a valuable Rolodex (remember those?) for your database and sphere of influence to leverage. Your value is emphasized when other people see you as having connections everywhere. Being the source of the source is also a way to limit liability, since it directs the consumer to the person with the answers and the consumer can ask questions directly of the subject matter expert and not ever say they got the info directly from you, in the event something goes awry.

A loan officer should also have excellent communication and let both agents know at what stage the loan is and set reasonable expectations about what will happen next and what timelines can be met.

They should also alert you (if you represent the buyer) right away if there are ever any issues with the loan. They should be ordering the appraisal immediately and honoring the closing date. If a deal closes late because the loan wasn't ready, with limited exception, that is unacceptable and a poor reflection on the loan officer.

Same goes for finding out in the middle of a transaction that the buyer should never have been pre-approved in the first place, because there's no way underwriting will sign off on the borrower/deal. Uncool, man!

Loan officers can also be a great resource for co-marketing campaigns and helping mitigate your costs. RESPA bars title companies from doing stuff like that, so make sure you check with any other state laws related to co-marketing to ensure you're operating within the bounds of the law.

If a loan officer offers you a lead-generation system that sends out ads on your behalf, make sure you're reviewing those ads to confirm they are law- and regulation-compliant. You don't want to get a nastygram from your local real estate division because you had noncompliant marketing out there and your only defense is "I didn't make the ad." Nope! Not good enough, bucko.

Big box banks (e.g., Wells Fargo, Bank of America, US Bank, etc.) have different guidelines than local lenders, which can sometimes make for more complicated loan approval processes, longer approval timelines (kiss that closing date goodbye), inability to fund a loan based on emailed copies of signed loan documents, and other inflexible restrictions which a local lender could accommodate. Not saying all national lenders are like that, and oftentimes it's the quality of the loan officer alone that can make the difference. Just be aware of such things as you're getting to know different loan officers and lending companies.

THE ATTORNEY PLUG: THEY GOTTA EAT, TOO

It's also highly advisable to have an experienced, respected real estate attorney on your team. Our industry is rife with liability, and agents can get into trouble all too easily. It pays to have someone you can lean on, someone you know will give you reliable, level-headed guidance when you think something is amuck, or if an unhappy principal to a transaction is threatening legal action. Deferring to an attorney usually comes after you've already gone through your broker and shizz is definitely hitting the fan.

DO YOU HAVE WARREN BUFFET ON SPEED DIAL?

Consider a financial advisor and a tax professional as teammates also. You need their services anyway, for proper financial and tax planning. Plus, you will likely have an opportunity to refer their services if your client doesn't have a CPA, or financial advisor, and needs tax advice, etc.

THE LITTLE BLACK BOOK

Throughout your transactions you'll need to find all sorts of vendors for things. Ask for referrals and then keep track of the ones you like and who did a good job. My little black book of vendors is a prized possession. I'm grateful for the library I've developed over the years; it not only comes in handy on our own deals, but it's really great to be able to help out another agent in my office who is looking for a vendor and needs a referral. I really appreciate when other agents have done that for me.

We can all do a google, but it's usually best to get a referral from someone you trust. When scheduling is an issue, or if it's a really unusual vendor you need and no one else has experienced that, Google can definitely be your friend, so never knock it. I leverage the internet all the time.

Think of this broad array of title and escrow officers, loan officers, landscapers, handymen, contractors, etc. as part of your overall team. You are all in service to the client, and you have a part to play in leaving the client with a stellar impression of you and the transaction. Happy clients are repeat clients.

Treating all the players in your transactions with respect and courtesy will go a long way to create strong working relationships and smoother deals. They'll also be more likely to bend over backward to make things happen for you because you are so great to work with. We're not generally motivated to go above and beyond for jerks who are disrespectful towards us.

THE COGS IN THE MACHINE (YOU'RE ONE, TOO)

Now for your internal team. If you're already thinking about how you can grow and create a team, you first need to have enough leads and business generation that you need help to efficiently and effectively process all those transactions and service all those clients.

The first position you should fill is admin. If your broker offers an in-house transaction coordinator, use them. It's expensive to pay an employee, and cash flow is a huge concern when you're new (it's important all the time, of course, but especially when your pipeline is skant). Delegate administrative tasks first so you can manage more lead generation.

If you're blessed with an overabundance of leads and you truly feel like you're drowning, then it's time to bring on another licensee to help you work those leads. Be careful when you step into the realm of teams or partnerships. If you're working with a friend or family member, you still need to create a plan for your partnership and what your exit strategy is if things don't work out—basically a business prenup.

How do you split your costs and commissions? Maybe you need to talk to a business attorney, a CPA, and your broker to help you craft a clear and concise business agreement that covers all your buns and bases. Buns and Bases—that's a great name for a law firm.

Now things are really hopping on your team and you're feeling bogged down with marketing tasks and the little bit of transaction coordination that's still on your plate. Now it's time to bring on another administrative person. They don't need to be licensed, but you do need to be clear on what an unlicensed assistant can and cannot do in your state.

Have them take over all transaction management (save the fee from the in-house coordinator) and your marketing programs (expired campaigns, drip campaigns, social media posts, newsletters, etc.) and help them elevate to being an invaluable member of the team through proper training. Don't drop them in a chair, give them a brief overview of the tasks at hand, and then wish them luck. Remember that awesome, painstakingly thorough manual you've been developing? Use that in your trainings so the new recruit has a proper handoff from one-on-one training to being guided by the manual you made. Also, having this new employee be your personal administrative assistant is a huge help, too, since they can help manage your appointments, designation and license renewals, and such. The more you get to focus on dollar-productive activities, the better. Don't get bogged down in the daily do.

Teams can look a lot of ways, and what you have to determine early on is what kind of focus you want to have (buyers or sellers). It's not to say that you can't or won't work with both types of clients, but it helps you have focus and direction for your overall business if you make a decision on this first.

It's more expensive to be a listing agent (think about marketing costs), but buyers can be more labor intensive, since you need to be in the field more, showing property and likely working more weekends to host open houses, accommodate out-of-area buyers or buyers with tough workweek schedules.

Since you know what your income goal is, you can structure a team you can afford and that will help you reach your goals. You've also thought about your funnels of business, and thus you can create programs, which your team can help you execute, to attract more leads in those specific funnels.

Small teams can also be high-producing teams. It's a combo of efficiency and desired market segment. You can easily be a team of two or three, with one primary salesperson as the team lead, and still gross $1,000,000 in commissions per year. The workload on the team lead will be higher, but if that person's lifestyle and drive can withstand that workload, then gods bless them. Go get 'em, tiger!

Similarly, you can have a small team (4 people or less) and focus on luxury or an above-average price in your market, do fewer deals per year, but make the same amount of money as the other person who is doing twice as many deals, but all at a lower value.

You figure out what combo works for you and then create the systems and procedures you need to attract and properly service that volume and those clients.

Side note: if you are thinking of focusing on luxury real estate, do yourself a favor and get your CLHMS designation. It stands for Certified Luxury Home Marketing Specialist. The classes you take to get that designation will help you communicate with luxury clients in their language and also market their homes better than the average bear. Plus it shows that you went the extra mile to get the education needed to help you meet their "special needs." It could be a boost to you in a listing appointment where the other agents vying for the listing don't have that point of distinction.

Speaking of designations, there are tons of them out there. While having too many after your name can result in unintelligible "alphabet soup," having ones that specifically pertain to your focused market segment are great. They help set you apart from the competition and keep you on top of your game. Same for specialty associations. Once you get a designation, take advantage of all the tools and education they offer. Get your money's worth out of it!

WELCOME ABOARD!

Tips on hiring:

1. Hire slowly, fire quickly. You do not have room on your team for bad employees or the time to wait for them to get their act together.

2. Write clear, concise, and specific job postings. Get clear on the job description first. This not only makes your ad easy for candidates to understand, it also offers clear expectations of their responsibilities when they join the team and provides a context for creating reasonable performance goals and guidelines.

3. Do a phone interview first. Start with some basic questions to get a feel for the candidate and look for any red flags. If you like what you hear over the phone, proceed to the next step. If not, thank them for their time and move on.

4. Set an in-person interview. This is when you get a chance to see how they dress (does it match your expectations of professionalism and your set dress code, if you care to have one?), how they carry themselves, how timely they are. This is also a good opportunity to talk about compensation and bonus structure, if you have one. If you need guidance on what to pay someone, you can either ask your broker (since they are paying receptionists, etc. and should have a good sense about fair wages) or you can do a google and check out some rate guides to ensure you're not overpaying or underpaying your employee.

5. Have the candidate do a few small tests like spelling and grammar (they will be emailing your clients and writing letters for you. You don't want those going out with "your welcome." So embarrassing.) Even a simple math test is good. You can go the extra mile and have them do computer tests to show their typing and Microsoft Office Suite skills. If a candidate says they have experience being a real estate assistant and they know how to use MLS, have them prove it! Their level of experience might not be what you expect or want.

6. Here's an interesting step in the hiring process you might want to consider: taking them out to dinner or lunch and inviting their significant other to join them. You will be bringing yours, too, if you have one. It's an opportunity to get a glimpse into the stability of their personal life. If they have crazy drama going on at home, it will more than likely spill into their work life. Now, everyone has stuff going on, so it's not to say they have to have some perfectly dull personal life where no waves are ever made—that seems weird, too. But, if the candidate is dealing with a ton of crazy shizz and it affects their focus and effectiveness at work, you want to avoid that can of worms.

7. Once you bring on the hire, have a probationary period (60-90 days) where the new employee is clear on the expectations, understands that their position is not permanent

until they've successfully gone through the probationary period, and knows what success looks like. You can even start them at a lower rate of pay and have a built-in "raise" when the probationary period has ended successfully.

8. Note about bonuses: it's okay, and more affordable, to keep your employees at a lower base rate of pay IF you have a secure and reasonable bonus structure in place. They can end up making a lot more money, and it's tied to the team's overall success, which is good for you as the owner/team leader.

As your internal team grows, take the time to introduce them to your external team of preferred vendors, so everyone knows who is who and can continue the same fantastic working relationships you've taken the time to build. It's a beautiful thing.

Chapter 12

SELF-CARE

*Avoiding burnout ... budget for vacations ... weekends
... exercise ... protecting your personal boundaries*

Now that you have a well-oiled moneymaking machine, how are you making sure that you are taken care of and able to be on point for your clients and your team? Self-care is real, y'all. If you choose to roll your eyes and push ahead, burning the midnight oil, you are on the fast track to burnout, my friend. It's not a good look, and it can destroy what you're building.

Bring out your budget; look for that line item titled "vacation." Now, go take one. You don't have to be jet-setting to the French Riviera or something, just do what you can to get away from work, clear your mind, have fun, and recharge.

When you go on vacation, two things will happen.

1. Offers will magically appear on your stale listings while you're away, or a buyer who has been taking forever to make a decision about writing an offer will suddenly be ready, and your awesome team (or backup person) will take care of all that in your absence.

2. You will come back to work refreshed and ready to see challenges with a new perspective, and be grateful for what you have, which will inherently bring you business.

All good things.

Now, vacations and getaways are great, but your budget only allows for so many per year. Thinking on another level, do you guard your weekends (whatever days you designate "weekends" to be) and free time? Caveat always being the accommodation of out-of-area buyers and hand-holding needed for sensitive deals. Aside from that, you don't have to work every weekend just for the sake of working. That also leads to burnout. Remember: burnout is bad.

Do you plan fun things on your weekends? Are you into outdoor activities or sports? Are you more introverted and need quiet time alone or with your family to read, rest, and build a birdhouse? Do you exercise regularly? Scientific studies have shown that exercise increases energy and focus—both of which you need to be successful. If you're dragging ass and distracted every day, your ship will crash into the rocks.

The beauty of exercise is that you can do it whenever you want! You can work out at 5:00 a.m. and be one of those people, or you can work out at 8:00 p.m. and then fight crime after. Vigilante justice! I kid. The point is, you can fit it in whenever it works for you. Heck, that could just mean taking a 30-minute walk at lunchtime around your office or a nearby park. It doesn't have to be some insane CrossFit-training regimen fit for Ninja Warrior prep.

I also find exercise helpful when you're involved in a rough deal and under a lot of pressure or stress. Keep in mind that what we feel is all self-imposed. Our emotions feel very powerful and real. But our minds also have the power to put things in context, be objective, and allow us to focus on the tasks at hand and leave behind all the messy, emotional stuff that has us freaking out in the first place. Taking a walk or busting through a tough workout can help you shake off all the anger, fear, etc., see things from a new perspective, and give you the insight you need to approach your next steps and conversations with more confidence and clarity.

There's almost nothing worse than being in the middle of an emotion storm and lashing out at another agent—or even your client—in a fit of rage, or making decisions and giving advice while in that mindset. Holy bad idea, Batman! That will just make things so much worse, even if you feel "better" in the moment for telling someone off. In the end, you'll kick yourself for throwing a tantrum, and it'll likely result in a complaint against you, at least to your broker, who can hopefully knock some sense into you.

Don't be that person. When things are stressing you out, step away from the catalyst and breathe some fresh air. Let your lizard brain disconnect so you can have all your mental faculties at your disposal.

My dad has been through burnout more than once, and it isn't pretty. My broker has also experienced burnout twice, and now she is committed to a new structure in her life and business that keeps burnout at bay. You could also be in real estate now because you got to the point of burnout in another industry. Don't let history repeat itself. Let their experiences of burnout (or the memory of yours) help you avoid the same pitfall in your real estate practice and create those structures for yourself now, so you don't have to experience burnout for yourself, or experience it again.

Chapter 13

WHAT'S NEXT?

Well my friend, this is where I leave you, for now. You have created a solid foundation from which to build your real estate empire, whether that is just you being Han Solo, the lone wolf of real estate—kicking ass and taking names, maybe with one steady co-pilot to help you man the ship—or if it's being the leader of a huge team that has their eye on world domination. Either way, you are poised for success because you've taken the time to think things through, approach your foray into real estate as a business, create a proper budget and a business plan, and have a vision for your future.

You're already better than every other new licensee out there. See how awesome you are?

If you ever find yourself running off the rails, or think you are about to, get out your business plan. Read through your mission, inspiration, culture, beliefs, and expectations. Get reconnected to your "why." Remind yourself what is important to you and what you're committed to. Make sure you have all the right people on your bus and surrounding you in life. Kick off anyone that's injecting negativity into your business or your life and is not on board with your culture.

If you find yourself feeling bored or stifled, get creative and innovative. Have you reached a point where you need to branch out from what you've been doing? Has all the experience you've accumulated shown you that your true passion and purpose within the real estate field lies somewhere else? Do you want to be a coach or mentor to new agents? Do you want to be a broker? Do you want to be the president of your local board or seek higher levels of service within the industry?

On the other hand, if you love the sales game and are creating a team, how do you maintain or grow what you're building? How do you scale it down or sell it as a means of retirement? How do you build a team that allows you to remain involved, keep an income stream, but step away from day-to-day operations and being the source of all the business? How do you replicate and expand?

The world is your oyster. Just define what you want and take steps to get there. The universe will meet you halfway. Don't be afraid to reinvent yourself. Be afraid of stagnating.

All that juicy stuff I'm saving for my next book. For now, just focus on being the best real estate professional you can, and then we'll meet again when you're ready for the next level.

I can't wait for you to share your successes and for you to be a phenomenal, shining star in your real estate market.

To stay in the conversation about elevating your game, make sure to subscribe to my podcast, *Do It and Be Glad You Did*. I love connecting with listeners and sharing your insights on the show.

Good luck!

ACKNOWLEDGMENTS

Big thank you to: Adam, Lori, and Jarod for being the most amazing creative team ever. To Alex Ellison for introducing me to Adam in the first place. To Josh for being my social justice warrior; to Bryce for being my cheerleader and head trash squasher; to Tova for being my best friend; and to Chris Webster who helps get my voice out there every week. To Renee Luce for taking me out to lunch, where inspiration struck to write a book. And to Kimberly Elliott for helping me conquer my fears, getting Larry to shup up, and believing in my ability to create something incredible.

AUTHOR BIO

Shauna Ganes is a Nevada real estate licensee and Realtor. Shauna cut her teeth on short sales in 2008 and learned the real estate business when being a professional was the difference between surviving in a down market and finding a new job. She brings her practical real estate experience to the forefront as a means of helping prospective real estate licensees be the best they can, while uplifting the reputation and image of real estate agents across the board. She is the host of *Do It and Be Glad You Did*, a podcast for real estate professionals committed to elevating their game. It's available on all major podcast platforms. The show is a weekly opportunity to stay in the conversation about enhancing your professionalism and learning best practices.

For updated info on the show, search for "Do It and Be Glad You Did" on Facebook, and if you want to find out more on Shauna's latest shenanigans, go to www.shaunaganes.com.

Shauna lives in Reno, NV, with her phenomenal husband and two adorable children. She loves karaoke, dancing, and experimenting in the kitchen.

www.ingramcontent.com/pod-product-compliance
Lightning Source LLC
Chambersburg PA
CBHW020157200326
41521CB00006B/403